The Essential
BARTENDER'S
How to Create
Truly Great
Cocktails
GUIDE

The Essential
BARTENDER'S
How to Create
GUIDE
Truly Great
Cocktails

ROBERT HESS

Mud Puddle Books
NEW YORK

The Essential Bartender's Guide:
How to Make Truly Great Cocktails
by Robert Hess

© 2008 by Mud Puddle Books, Inc.

Published by
Mud Puddle Books, Inc.
54 W. 21st Street
Suite 601
New York, NY 10010
info@mudpuddlebooks.com

ISBN: 978-1-7418-2847-4

Design by Libby VanderPloeg
For complete photographic credits please see page 216.

Printed in China

Table of Contents

Introduction

Cocktails have been enjoyed for more than 200 years, and throughout those 200 years the word *cocktail* has consistently conjured up different images for different people. A confusion, yes, but a tasty one.

The history of cocktails begins with just a few drinks created by the bartenders of the day. They had such names as the Whiskey Cocktail, Brandy Cocktail, Gin Cocktail, Fancy Whiskey Cocktail, Fancy Brandy Cocktail and Fancy Gin Cocktail. For a while these were just about the extent of available cocktails. But it didn't take long for this simple list to expand to dozens, then hundreds, then thousands of different drinks created by the imaginations of the countless bartenders around the world.

Today, the number of different cocktails available is so extensive that keeping abreast of the latest trends can be a daunting challenge to even the most knowledgeable bartender. So it's no wonder that the average consumer may be overwhelmed and intimidated by the variety of choices available. Is it any surprise that many of us order the same tried-and-true drink over and over again no matter what bar or country we're in? It's almost like going to a Chinese restaurant and ordering a hamburger without even looking at the menu.

Wine and beer stay nicely within a certain range of flavors making it relatively easy for consumers to match their particular tastes. Cocktails, however, can span an extremely broad spectrum of flavors. This could lead us to settle into a comfort zone relying on a very limited set of drinks. But to do so would be to cut off an infinite world of possibilities. The

BALE OF HAY SALOON   VIRGINIA CITY, MONT.

information and the recipes included here are intended to open the doors of discovery leading to new and exciting drinks to try at your favorite restaurant or bar as well as to make at home for the delight of your family and friends. Bartenders, both experienced and fledgling, may also find new avenues of inspiration.

It wasn't that long ago that cocktails were barely more than a gimmicky and showy alcohol delivery vehicle. They were presented in a dizzying range of flavors and colors that would embarrass a peacock. The construction of a drink was focused more on being provocative and trendsetting than in creating a product reflecting the craftsmanship and culinary ability of the bartender. Thankfully, in recent years, things have been changing. There has been a notable resurgence in bartenders with both the knowledge and the skills to use the wide range of ingredients at their disposal to create new cocktails of subtlety and inspiration. In addition, this new breed of bartenders are able to exquisitely execute the classic cocktails of the past in a way that has not been seen for nearly a hundred years.

The goal of this book is to present bartenders, both home and professional, with the information needed to really understand the cocktail and how to properly prepare the best drinks possible. Given straightforward information on preparation and ingredients as well as a touch of the evolutionary history of the cocktail, you can mix a world-class drink. Understanding will take the confusion out of the word cocktail.

At the same time, you'll uncover some hidden truths about the cocktail, and hopefully a new found appreciation for what a cocktail can be when properly prepared. You'll soon recognize bartenders who have the necessary training and craftsmanship to draw out the culinary nuances of the drinks you order.

Let the journey begin!

Cocktail Insights and History

What is--and is not--a cocktail? Seems like a simple question. We've all seen those neon signs outside a bar promoting "Cocktails." Likewise we've seen menus at lounges and restaurants which list a dozen or more drinks on their "Martini Menu." We might see a happy hour menu which mentions discounted prices on "Well Drinks." We hear of "High Balls," "Mixed Drinks" and perhaps "Sours." Often it appears that the differences between these items are elusive. Drinks are lumped together in a general bucket and labeled according to their perceived customer appeal.

There is, however, fairly specific differences to each of these and it's just as important for the bartender to understand these differences as it is for a chef to understand the differences between a stock, a broth and a consommé. Such differences may not be immediately apparent to the consumer and may appear at first to be insignificant, but they play a crucial role in understanding the craft of bartending and the products which can be produced.

Havana, Cuba 1931:
Sloppy Joe Jr., age four, mixing his first champagne cocktail at his father's world-famed bar.

History Lesson

One way to understand mixed drinks in general, and specifically cocktails, is to look briefly at their history and evolution.

Cocktails use distilled spirits as their foundation, and distilled spirits use fermented wines and other products as their building blocks. Therefore, the history of the cocktail needs to begin with a brief look at the history of fermentation.

Fermentation

Fermentation is a natural process, so natural in fact that it takes about as much effort to prevent it than it does to produce it. Leave any starch or sugar bearing liquid around and fermentation will take place on its own. Wine that has been dealcoholized will, under normal circumstances, still have $^1/_{10}$ of one percent alcohol in it, less than a fresh-squeezed glass of orange juice.

Fermentation has been known for thousands of years. It's easy to imagine that once upon a time someone left a little gruel or mashed up berries out when he was interrupted by an extended hunting trip, only to return to find that his forgotten meal had slightly changed character. A taste produced interesting, if not downright spiritual, effects.

It's not a great leap to go from these early accidents to producing products similar to the beers and wines we have today, although it's not hard to imagine that the earliest attempts might have seemed more medicinal than enjoyable. Before quality can be controlled in a process, a full understanding of the process itself is necessary. Only then can you know precisely how quality can be repeated and improved upon.

It wasn't until the mid-1800s that yeast and the role it played in fermentation was first defined. Louis Pasteur, the extraordinary French chemist and microbiologist, was asked to find out why some batches of wine and beer go sour for no apparent reason. He soon discovered that yeast, a living organism, was responsible for fermentation and that it was not, as generally thought, the result of a chemical catalyst. He was able to determine that different strains of yeast produced different results and that allowing the yeasts to thrive too long would sour the product. Prior to this, wines, beers and even breads would be made without any concept of adding yeast at all. Instead the winemaker, brewmaster or baker simply relied—unknowingly—upon the naturally occurring yeasts in the air to produce the desired results. So, for several thousand years, the fermented product, which is the basis of distilled spirits, could often be of a questionable quality since the actual process which produced them was pretty much hit or miss.

Distillation

Distillation, unlike naturally occurring fermentation, takes place, for the most part, through human intervention. Simply put, distillation is a process used to separate the alcohol from the non-alcohol in a fermented product. To do so, it takes science.

We know that water freezes at 32°Fahrenheit (0°C) and alcohol freezes at -173° Fahrenheit (-114°C). Using this information, one basic method of distillation is to take a liquid containing alcohol, water and other ingredients and get it cold enough to start to freeze. In this case, the water will freeze and the alcohol will remain a liquid. This will allow you to strain out the alcohol. Unfortunately, the other ingredients may not freeze and, depending on what they are, they may reach unhealthy concentrations.

A better use of science to solve this problem is to go in the opposite direction. Instead of applying cold, we apply heat. Water boils at 212°Fahrenheit (100°C) while alcohol boils at 173 degrees Fahrenheit (78.5°C). When a liquid boils, it turns to steam. If you capture that steam and allow it to cool, it will turn back into a liquid. Now, when a liquid is a mixture of one liquid (water) that boils at 212° and another boils at 173°, the actual point that the liquid will boil is somewhere between the two. The vapors that come off will be a combination of the liquids with a much higher concentration of the liquid with the lower boiling point (the alcohol) than the one with the higher boiling point (the water). So if you put a pot of wine on the stove and bring it to a boil, the vapors that come off will contain more alcohol than the liquid that is left in the pot. This is the

Pot stills at a Scottish Whisky distillery

basis of standard distillation.

The historical origins of distillation are fairly obscure. We know that the ancient Egyptians used distillation for perfumes, some of which may have been applied orally as a sort of breath freshener. Creating concentrated alcohol was not the intent. It wasn't until the mid-1400s when the concept of distillation was brought to what is now the United Kingdom that distilling a fermented product in order to concentrate the alcohols would come into its own. It may have been Ireland or Scotland that first introduced alcohol distillation, but since both produce wonderful products, it probably doesn't much matter.

While whiskies were being made in the U.K., France was happy enough with the wines it was producing. However, it's said that ingenious suppliers thought they could use distillation to create a wine concentrate to ship more wine in less space. They intended to reconstitute the wine on the other end by simply adding water. While this might have sounded good in theory, it didn't work well in actual practice. It was soon noted, however, that the wine concentrate had some interesting properties on its own, and thus brandy (*brandewijn* or "burnt wine") was created.

Why, in a book focused on cocktails, do we spend so much time discussing fermentation and distillation? Believe it or not, there is a very strong correlation between mixed drinks and distillation—and not just because distilled products are part of a mixed drink.

The Mixed Drink

Just as thousands of years of early wine and beer production were more luck than science, the early days of distillation were fairly hit or miss as well. While the euphoric side effects of the alcohol were desirable results, the taste made consumption a bitter pill to swallow. Beers and wines were increasing in their overall quality, but they were also bulky and costly to transport. Spirits on the other hand were far more concentrated and therefore a cheaper product to move around. Just as Mary Poppins tells us about the wonders of a spoonful of sugar, the early bartenders found it advantageous to augment the flavors of their "burnt wine" with water, sugar, juices and spices to make their "medicine" easier to take.

Originally, such a mixed drink might take the form of just about anything that could increase the palatability of the concentrated spirit. Over time, the evolving practice of mixing drinks began to not only take form but also take on various names as well. A "punch" was perhaps the most popular, being made from spirits, water, citrus, sugar, as well as various spices. The added ingredients did their job of masking the often poor quality of the base spirit used.

The creation of base recipes produced

a classification system for drinks. Among the classifications were drinks designated as a Fix, a Sour, a Fizz or a Daisy. Consumers would dictate what spirit was added to their drink by requesting a Brandy Fix, a Brandy Sour, a Brandy Fizz or a Brandy Daisy. At the same time, drinks began to ride the crest of fashion. Just as skirt length was dictated by fashion, the popularity of a certain drink would be dictated by fashion. And just as quickly as last season's runway designs, drinks could fall out of fashion.

Up to this point mixed drinks were known to consist of poor quality spirits and a base recipe to render those spirits palatable. The base recipe existed in several different categories which defined the style of drink. Things began to change and these changes would lead us to the cocktail.

Printed history from those days, especially relating to spirituous drink, is rather spotty. Currently, the earliest known reference to a drink referred to as a "*cocktail*" was recently uncovered by noted cocktail historian David Wondrich. The reference appeared on April 28, 1803, in *Farmer's Cabinet*, a newspaper out of Amherst, New Hampshire. The paper published a bit of humor disguised as a journal entry from an affluent young partygoer. In the entry he mentions that he "drank a glass of cocktail - excellent for the head." Since "cocktail" was not defined, we can assume that the

226
*Putting
a Big
Schooner
into the
Dock.*

Postcard, 1907

publishers felt it was already a well-established drink in the area, even if a relatively new one.

Three years later, in 1806, "cocktail" was mentioned in the *Balance and New Columbian Repository* out of Hudson, New York. In this case the term "cock-tail" is again tossed out without explanation. This time a quizzical reader writes to the editor to ask what this thing might be. A week later, Harry Crosswell, the editor, provided a slightly politically charged response which happened to also include the definition of the cocktail as being "… spirits of any kind, sugar, water, and bitters - it is vulgarly called a bittered sling…" He continued:

"(The cocktail) is supposed to be an excellent electioneering potion in as much as it renders the heart stout and bold, at the same time it fuddles the head. It is said also, to be of great use to a democratic candidate: because, a person having swallowed a glass of it, is ready to swallow anything else."

Political humor aside, this response provides the definition as well as the notion that the cocktail is the same thing as a sling with the addition of bitters. Well, you can't always believe what you read. This description isn't necessarily an accurate one.

In the early 1800s, a sling was a mixed drink in which water and a sweetening ingredient of one sort or another was added to help mask the poor spirits of the day.

The Bitter Truth

We now have the first indication that a pivotal ingredient in the cocktail is bitters. But what exactly are bitters? First, let's look at what was going on.

In those days, there were a variety of pressures being foisted on the average citizen, one of which was the notion of "temperance." Drunkenness was fairly common, partially due to the fact that water quality was quite suspect. To avoid contaminated water, many would drink hard cider or ale, both of which were seen as being safer than water.

However, the Temperance movement began preaching the ills of alcohol and the social problems brought about by drinking. There was a concerted effort to make it unfashionable to consume alcoholic beverages. For many, the solution to the problem came in the form of bitters. Bitters were a concentrate of various (supposedly) healthy herbs and botanicals. They just happened to be extracted using alcohol and were often bottled at 40% or higher alcohol by volume. This allowed "Father" to take his daily medicine—and get a nice buzz at the same time.

Bitters, however, were designed not to be tasty but medicinal. So, it doesn't come as much of a stretch to think that somebody might apply the same camouflage tricks to bitters as were being practiced with spirits. Soon, combining spirits and bitters along with additional flavor maskers would

Old bitters bottles

be seen as killing two birds with one stone. You could drink your medicine and enjoy it at the same time.

So, in the early 1800s, the cocktail would have some spirit as its base, a bit of bitters to allow it to pass as a "health tonic," enough sugar to clean up the taste and some added water to bring a little civility to the alcoholic burn. Ice was precious in those days, and it isn't likely that cocktails, or other drinks for that matter, would be chilled. It wasn't until the mid-1800s that ice would take the scene by storm, with iced drinks becoming a uniquely American delicacy.

Culinary Evolutions

All the celebrated cuisines of the world started out as a way to make the available food products palatable and digestible. Over time, through better understanding of both products and processes, the skills of the food preparer led to the discovery of ways to build upon and improve the flavors of the meals produced. As the realization evolved that eating could be more than just a survival technique, and as leisure time became available, the concept came about of food as an "art form" to be enjoyed, appreciated and studied came about. In other words, the concept of cuisine was born.

In the early 1800s similar culinary pressures were surrounding the cocktail. As a mixed drink, it was simply one of the many ways alcohol could be rendered consumable. Gradually, however, through better understanding of distillation, the quality of the spirits being produced was improving.

At the time, the common process of distilling was through the use of what is known as a "pot still." Better understanding of the process opened the door for advancements in distillation technology. A big leap came in 1831 when Aeneas Coffey patented his new "column still" (also known as patent still, continuous still and Coffey still). This new still made it possible to increase production of higher quality (and higher proof) spirits.

In addition to the advancements in distilling, a variety of other facets of the craft were also coming into focus.

Many American whiskey distillers were experimenting with aging their whiskies in oak casks. This helped mellow and deepen the flavor. It was also noticed that old oak barrels, which had their insides charred out to clean them, produced an even smoother whiskey. Around this time, we started to see the formation of companies to make whiskey and market them by brand name.

With the quality of spirits continually improving, it was no longer necessary to disguise their flavors with sugars, juices and spices. While this was happening, the role of the bartender was getting a bit of an overhaul. The bartender of the mid-1800s had evolved from the inn and tavern keeper of decades and even centuries prior. By now bartenders were becoming more artists than laborers, amazing their customers with the craftsmanship and often ornate presentation of the drinks they served.

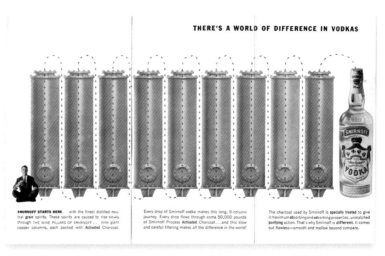

A column still process, as visualized in a vodka brochure called "The Nine Pillars of Smirnoff"

"Professor" Jerry Thomas

One of the most notable bartenders of the mid-1800s was Jerry Thomas. Thomas was born around 1830, and, by the time he was 16, he was already working as a barkeep in New Haven, Connecticut. In those days, bartenders had to serve an apprenticeship, much as potential chefs do today. Young Jerry Thomas faced many months, if not years, doing menial tasks at the beck-and-call of the head bartender. However, after a few years, Thomas, presumably weary of his chores, headed out to sea. He eventually landed in San Francisco during the great gold rush. He worked at several different bars, gaining both experience

Jerry Thomas making a Blue Blazer

and a reputation. Thomas continued to wander, however, making his way back to New Haven and eventually to New York City. Wherever he was, he was soon bitten by the travel bug and his wanderings never ceased. Over the years he would work in Charleston, Chicago, St. Louis, Keokuk (Iowa), New Orleans, Virginia City (Nevada) and, briefly, throughout Europe.

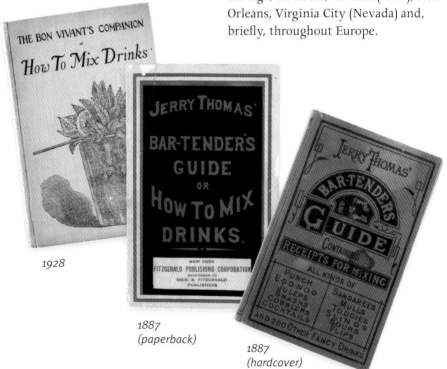

1928

1887 (paperback)

1887 (hardcover)

The Bon-Vivant's Companion

Jerry Thomas's lasting renown isn't for his traveling. In 1862 he published a bartender's guide simply called *How to Mix Drinks, or, The Bon-Vivant's Companion*. This is generally believed to be the very first collection of mixed drink recipes. For its day, the book is a comprehensive collection of recipes covering a wide variety of mixed drinks. For us, it's an extraordinary time capsule glimpse of what people were drinking back then. We've already talked about the evolution of mixed drink categories and that first and foremost in the minds of drinkers across the country was punch. Naturally Thomas begins his book with a large collection of punch recipes. He follows punch with sections containing recipes for:

EGGNOG DRINKS (generally with brandy, rum, milk, sugar and, at times, raw eggs)

JULEPS (sweet, syrupy drinks made from a variety of spirits, sugar and mint)

SMASHES (referred to as "a julep on a small plan," usually made with brandy, sugar, club soda, sugar and mint)

COBBLERS (wine or liqueur, sugar and fruit)

COCKTAILS (Thomas says, "The 'Cocktail' is a modern invention, and is generally used on fishing and other sporting parties, although some patients insist that it is good in the morning as a tonic.")

CRUSTAS (brandy, rum, lemon or lime juice, bitters; Thomas says, "The 'Crusta' is an improvement on the 'Cocktail'...")

MULLS (sweetened ale or wine flavored with spices and heated)

SANGAREES (sangria; wine, brandy, sugar, fruit juice and club soda)

TODDIES (sweetened hot water, alcohol and often spiced with cloves)

SLINGS (sweetened brandy, whiskey or gin, often flavored with lemon)

FIXES (alcohol of choice, sugar, lemon and water)

SOURS (generally whiskey, lemon or lime juice, sugar and maybe club soda)

FLIPS (alcohol of choice with beaten raw egg)

NEGUSES (wine, hot water, lemon juice, sugar and nutmeg)

SHRUBS (rum or brandy, fruit juice and sugar)

Clockwise, from top left: 1895, 1902, 1884, 1900

Thomas closes with a slightly random collection of "Fancy Drinks," "Miscellaneous Drinks" and "Temperance Drinks."

We should note that the category of "Cocktails" simply appears clustered in among various other categories, some of which you may have heard of before, but many of which you most likely have not. What's probably most interesting, however, is that in this very first bartender's guide, which was intended to be a complete collection of recipes which a bartender needed to know, there were only ten cocktail recipes.

The Cocktail Pulls Ahead

Over time the role of the cocktail as an important component of the bartender's repertoire grew significantly. This is readily apparent when we look at the new 1887 edition of Jerry Thomas's guide. Appearing 25 years after the original and two years after his death, the revised guide lists cocktails first while doubling the recipes to twenty.

Bartenders across the country, and more importantly, the customers they served, began to herald the cocktail as the king of the mixed drinks. The cocktail was seen to be uniquely positioned not as a masker of spirits but a celebrator of them.

Bitters were at the core of early cocktail recipes. Some early bitters were intended to be consumable liquids in their own right, but the bitters that became key tools to the bartender were the ones designed to be measured in simple dashes to accent flavor rather than being a major flavor element in their own right. In this manner they should be treated as salt might in soup. A soup without any salt will taste slightly flat and bland, and one with too much salt will taste… well… salty. But when used in proper amounts, the salt will heighten and energize the other flavors. The same can be said of bitters; they accentuate and blend together the flavors of a cocktail without making the cocktail taste bitter.

A barman pours a drink at London's Savoy Hotel bar, 1926.

It was this little bit of culinary magic, which came into existence at just the right time, which allowed the cocktail to capture the imagination and taste buds of the consuming public.

As we've already seen, the original cocktail recipe featured spirits of any kind, sugar, water and bitters. This was the essence of cocktails for many decades. In Jerry Thomas's books, he listed drinks such as the Whiskey Cocktail, Brandy Cocktail and Gin Cocktail. These were little more than the base spirit sweetened with simple syrup and sometimes a bit of orange curaçao and a dash of bitters, all mixed with ice. His recipes also listed Fancy Whiskey Cocktail, Fancy Brandy Cocktail and Fancy Gin Cocktail. Actually these were precisely the same drinks as the first list. They earned the adjective "fancy" by being served in a fancy wine glass, the rim of which had been rubbed with a piece of lemon peel.

In the 19th century, the bartender's arsenal was somewhat limited, particularly when compared to today. Looking through published recipes of the time, you basically see the use of four base spirits (whiskey, brandy, gin and rum), some wines, flavored syrups, juices, fruit, sugar and bitters. Other products such as tequila and vodka existed but hadn't yet gained any popularity in America.

With the appearance of vermouth behind the bar in the later half of the 1800s, a new style of cocktail was born. Initially vermouth was added to the existing cocktail formula. Soon, however, imaginative bartenders created new cocktails that no longer contained any sugar or syrups. In part, this was due to the use of sweet vermouth. Later, when dry vermouth was used instead of sweet, it was discovered that these new cocktails worked quite well without the sweeteners of the past. Among the new drinks, we encounter the first Manhattan which was followed shortly after by the first Martini. These drinks quickly became fashionable. It seemed like everyone wanted to be seen with a Manhattan or a Martini in hand.

Turning the Century

As we move into the 20th century, we begin to see cocktails served and promoted at all of the world's finest hotels. Bartenders trained for years in preparation and presentation. Cocktails are served in barware and glassware that is elegant, ornate and captivating. The bars themselves become veritable cathedrals to libation. The image is easy to conjure: ornately carved wood, elegantly etched glass, fine silver and crisply appointed barmen serving drinks to gentlemen dressed in their finest suites. The cocktail had come of age, and its culinary position was firmly established.

Or was it?

Dark Times Ahead

The temperance movement hadn't gone away. It was still trying to provide moral enlightenment and convince the populace about the evils of alcohol. However, where once the movement was fine with mere moderation and the limiting of alcoholic consumption, it was now demanding total abstinence as the only solution to all of society's ills.

On December 18, 1917, Congress passed the 18th Amendment, which would, if ratified by three-quarters of the states, make prohibition part of the U.S. Constitution. Ratification came on January 16th, 1919, after 36 states approved the amendment. A year later, January 16, 1920, the 18th Amendment became law. The provisions of the amendment made it illegal to manufacture, sell or transport "intoxicating liquors within, the importation thereof into, or the exportation thereof from the United States and all territory subject to the jurisdiction thereof." This appeared to provide the social reforms that the temperance unions desired—at least for a while.

Prohibition was expected to end drinking in America for all time. Bartenders of the day had two choices: either flee to Europe if they wished to continue their trade or find other jobs if they wished to stay in America.

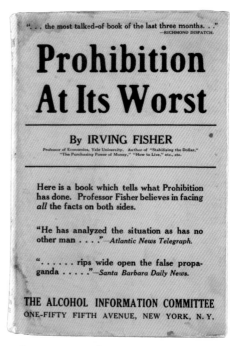

"... the most talked-of book of the last three months. .." —RICHMOND DISPATCH.

Prohibition At Its Worst

By IRVING FISHER
Professor of Economics, Yale University. Author of "Stabilizing the Dollar," "The Purchasing Power of Money," "How to Live," etc., etc.

Here is a book which tells what Prohibition has done. Professor Fisher believes in facing *all* the facts on both sides.

"He has analyzed the situation as has no other man . . . ."—*Atlantic News Telegraph.*

". . . . . . rips wide open the false propaganda . . . ."—*Santa Barbara Daily News.*

THE ALCOHOL INFORMATION COMMITTEE
ONE-FIFTY FIFTH AVENUE, NEW YORK, N. Y.

The New Saloon

The results of Prohibition were immediate. Liquor consumption dropped, public drunkenness declined and now-illegal alcohol was so expensive that it was out of the reach of the average worker. However, this was destined to change. It didn't happen immediately, but, as we know, where there's a will, there's a way. Over the course of a few years a new style of drinking establishment appeared on the scene: the speakeasy.

Speakeasies were clandestine establishments providing an alcoholic release to the mounting pressures of the day. For the consumer, this was a great step backward. Many of the spirits available were once again of questionable quality, and the staff

Customers enjoying drinks at a speakeasy, 1920s

serving drinks rarely had any formal training in the culinary arts that bartenders were so proudly practicing just a few short years before. We can only hazard a guess at the quality of the drinks served but the stories and recipes that emerged at this time don't instill much confidence.

All was not gloomy, however. There was one major change during this time that could be seen as a positive advancement. Prior to Prohibition, saloons and cocktail lounges were primarily a refuge for men. On the other hand, speakeasies were open to all comers. Not only did women enjoy a newfound freedom, but men discovered that they appreciated their company. Had it not been for Prohibition, who knows how long it would have taken bars to go co-ed.

Out the Other Side

Prohibition, as we all know, was a failure. Not only did it fail to bring

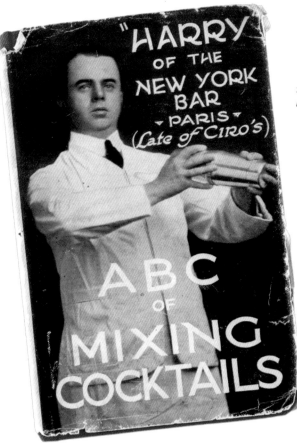

1922
by Harry McElhone

about the expected social and moral reforms that the temperance unions were fighting for, but by virtually all accounts, it made things even worse. On February 20th, 1933, Congress passed the 21st Amendment repealing the 18th Amendment. On December 5, 1933, when Utah became the 36th state to ratify the new amendment, it was official: America's dry period was over.

I often refer to Prohibition as the "Great Cocktail Lobotomy." During this time, one hundred years of the advancements in the art and skill of mixing drinks (mixology) were all but forgotten. Once again, cocktails were simply mixed drinks designed to disguise the poor quality spirits used and as a way to aid the intoxication of the customer. All dreams of culinary appreciation vanished.

Prior to Prohibition, the making of cocktails were left to professionals. Published bar guides were primarily intended for bartenders. With bars closed during Prohibition, it was common for people to have private cocktail parties at home, mixing drinks using whatever tools they could find around the house. Cocktail shakers were designed so they could hide in plain sight. As soon as prohibition ended, a massive number of cocktail recipe guides aimed at the general public appeared along with a flood of sophisticated, stylish barware clearly designed to compliment home décor while aiding home entertaining.

The bartenders of this post-Prohibition era were likely to be the same bartenders who had been working during Prohibition. This meant that their training was limited. Since they continued to approach mixed drinks as a masquerade rather than a celebration, how long would it take to rediscover the fine art of mixed drinks?

1927

Exotic Escapes

The period just after Prohibition produced a development in the evolution of the cocktail that shone with potential. Surprisingly enough, it probably would not have occurred if it weren't for Prohibition itself.

Remember, not only was alcohol illegal throughout the county, the manufacture of American whiskey was also illegal. When Prohibition was repealed, American whiskey couldn't pop back onto the shelves as if there weren't a 13-year manufacturing time lag. Whiskies had to be aged for several years, but even before

there's an aging process, all the whiskey distilleries had to reopen and restart their processes. The shortage meant that American whiskey was in high demand.

On the other hand, the manufacturing of rum from the Caribbean had never ceased and there was plenty to be had. To cope with the abundance of product, bar or liquor merchants often required customers to buy a case of rum for every American whiskey bottle purchased. It's not hard to imagine the result of this policy. There was a glut of rum on the market and bartenders needed to figure out how to use it.

Tiki Revolution

Enter the Tiki Bar. Consumers may have preferred American whiskey, but it was scarce. Since rum was plentiful,

1961

might be seen as tacky and kitschy, they actually represent a bold level of evolution in culinary drinks. Their general format was more akin to the classic punch (spirit, citrus, sweetener, spice, water), but the craftsmanship exhibited in the flavor profiles and the dedication of the bartenders who made the drinks was in line with craftsmanship of bartenders before Prohibition.

Unfortunately, as the years progressed, the model developed by Don Beach and Victor Bergeron was picked up by restaurant owners who couldn't see the exotic artistry beyond the façade and so what should have been seen as masterful craftsmanship eventually deteriorated into artificial kitsch.

Losing Our Way

The 1960s and 1970s were not happy times in the history of mixed drinks. The outside world looked to distance itself from the "establishment" and embrace the "here and now." It didn't take long for this attitude to pervade cocktail culture. Contemporary drinkers identified more with sweetened fortified wines from California, at least when they weren't self-medicating on other products. The Martini was seen as passé and part of the gentrified past.

All this changed as we entered the 1980s. Suddenly retro was the rage and the Martini became the symbol of retro libations. Unfortunately, challenging

it needed to become fashionable. So, to make rum appealing, it was promoted to be both foreign and exotic. Serve this new delight in an appropriately designed exotic appearing restaurant or bar, you suddenly have the illusion of an immediate vacation through the course of an evening's meal.

Don Beach was the originator of the overall concept. His "Don the Beachcomber" line of restaurants were followed in due course by Victor Bergeron and his "Trader Vic's" chain. While the cocktails and trappings often associated with these restaurants

1967

cocktails popular prior to Prohibition still hadn't made a comeback. Instead, overly sweet simplified drinks and overly sour mixes veiling their base alcohols continued to dominate. By serving drinks in the iconic "V" shaped cocktail glass, it was possible to maintain the illusion of elegance and the dignity of the classic Martini.

Resurgence

All was not lost. By the late 1990s, an awareness of classic cocktails emerged. Bartenders began to seek out both recipes and ingredients that had long been out of circulation. By using new technologies such as the internet, bartenders and customers around the world were able to gather and easily exchange information, insights and ideas. Old cocktail books, once worth little more than spare change in a used bookstore, are suddenly selling for hundreds of dollars on online auction sites.

Bitters, the quintessential cocktail ingredient, returned to common use. The lonely bottle of Angostura bitters, which was rarely seeing any use, is joined by several other brands as well as specialty bitters made by bartenders themselves.

Not only are the Manhattan, Old Fashioned and the true Martini now getting more appreciation, but other long forgotten drinks from the Golden Age of Cocktails reappear on cocktail menus around the world. The Aviation, Pegu Club, Clover Club, Last Word, Pisco Sour, Derby, Jack Rose, Rob Roy and countless others are reintroduced to an eagerly awaiting public.

Bartending Basics

The cocktail can, and should, be seen as a cuisine and the bartender should be seen as playing the same role as the chef. Instead of the raw materials a chef uses, a bartender uses spirits, cordials, vermouths, bitters and juices to build balanced and complimentary flavors to serve. But unlike most chefs, a bartender is expected to perform his or her duties right in front of the guests while being the consummate host. The world's best bartenders do not achieve stature simply based on the quality of the drinks they prepare. Reputations take into account personality, charm, presence and the ability to politely interact, no matter how busy, with guests.

This isn't meant to make the cocktail sound like something only a trained professional can make. In fact, all you need to make great drinks at home is an interest. The same skills a professional bartender relies upon are easily understood and utilized by the home bartender. Whether you are simply mixing a couple of drinks for yourself or hosting a cocktail party among friends, there is no reason why the quality of the drinks can't rival or surpass what might be found in the best cocktail lounges in the city. With the proper knowledge, skill, tools and ingredients, anyone will be able to create great cocktails at home.

Cocktails and Other Mixed Drinks

Savvy bartenders and their customers realize that the cocktail is just one of many categories of drinks lumped together under the broader banner of *mixed drink*. Just as it is important for a chef to understand the differences between a soufflé, custard, pudding and quiche, a true bartender needs to know the various types of mixed drinks if he or she truly wants to master the craft.

Just as the term *pudding* has come to refer to various dishes over the centuries, mixed drink styles are open to misunderstanding. Here is a list of styles and terms which will, hopefully, provide some insight to both the common and obscure forms that mixed drinks can take.

Some of these categories are no longer commonly found, but with the resurgence of interest in rediscovering many of the classic mixed drinks, you might just start seeing them crop up again.

Circa 1930

Buck

It might take more than a quick glance at various bartender manuals to differentiate a Buck from a Rickey, a Collins or a Fizz. Traditionally, however, a Buck should use ginger ale instead of club soda for carbonation. The ginger ale also provides sweetening and so no sugar is added. A Buck is the combination of spirit, ginger ale and lemon juice in a tall ice-filled glass.

> *For an example, see:*
> •*Gin Buck*

Cobbler

In its day, the Cobbler was *the* drink and its relatively simple construction of spirit, sugar and fruit mixed thoroughly with ice and served with straws was fairly groundbreaking. When the Cobbler first appeared in the 1830s, the use of ice and drinking straws was new and novel. While it's true that the modern paper straw wasn't patented until 1888, straws used fifty years earlier were just what the name says: straw. Usually the dried hollow stalk of rye, cut to length, would be served with the Cobbler, perhaps the first drink to call for its use. The name "cobbler" is thought to come from the small chunks of ice filling the drink like cobblestones used in paving.

> *For an example, see:*
> •*Brandy Cobbler*

Cocktail

The cocktail, as we've already seen, was initially defined as "spirits of any kind, sugar, water and bitters." This was a pretty safe definition until the later half of the 19th century when cocktails might have the sugar replaced by a fortified wine like vermouth or augmented with a little citrus. Bitters, however, would still be at the core of almost every cocktail, at least until Prohibition.

For an example, see:
•*Old Fashioned*

Collins

Collins is a sour served in a fairly tall glass with ice and club soda. The drink is usually made by stirring lemon juice, sweetener and spirit in an ice-filled glass topped with club soda. Today, Collins is best known in the form of the gin-based Tom Collins.

For an example, see:
•*Tom Collins*

Cooler

Perhaps the hardest part about a Cooler is the presentation of its garnish. This is also what differentiates it from what might otherwise be called a highball. The garnish used is a long continuous spiral made of a whole lemon, lime and/or orange peel placed in a Collins glass before adding ice and spirit topped off with club soda.

For an example, see:
•*Remsen Cooler*

Crusta

For the most part a Crusta is a gussied up cocktail. Jerry Thomas's recipe simply took a fancy cocktail and added a dash of lemon juice to it. He then served it in a sugar-rimmed glass (hence the name Crusta) and garnished it with a wide spiral slice of lemon peel. Compared to the cocktail, the Crusta, first appearing in New Orleans around 1850, never quite made it to the big time.

For an example, see:
•*Bourbon Crusta*
•*Brandy Crusta*

Daisy

The Daisy represents a slight modification of the Fix, both drinks being a single serving variation of a punch. The key difference with a Daisy, however, is that it uses either grenadine or raspberry syrup as its sweetener. Citrus juice and a spirit would be added to the syrup. This would be poured into a goblet filled with shaved or crushed ice and then garnished with a variety of fruits and berries.

For an example, see:
•*Gin Daisy*

Eggnog

We all know eggnog as a traditional Christmastime drink. Unfortunately our disposition toward eggnog may be colored by the horrid mixture that comes out of cardboard cartons.

However, traditional eggnog is made with some type of spirit (rum or brandy most preferred), eggs, milk and sugar. If served cold it would be mixed with ice; if served hot in a mug, it would have hot water added to it.

For an example, see:
•*Eggnog*

Fix

Sometimes there is neither the time nor the number of people to warrant a bowl of punch. In such cases you'd order a Fix, kind of a punch for one. Originally made by combining sugar, citrus, water and spirits, the Fix gradually evolved to feature a flavored syrup--usually pineapple--instead of plain sugar. It would be poured into a glass filled with shaved or crushed ice and then garnished with a variety of fruits and berries. Although the Fix was a key component of a bartender's repertoire prior to Prohibition, it has all but disappeared since then.

For an example, see:
•*Gin Fix*

Fizz

It's easy to confuse a Fizz with a Collins since the ingredients are essentially the same. The Fizz has, however, some slight differences. In a Fizz, the spirit, sweetener and citrus should be shaken first with ice before straining it into an ice-filled glass. It's then topped with club soda, ideally from a charged soda siphon to add a nice bubbly fizz.

Another difference is that, unlike the Collins, there are possible variations of the Fizz. For example, a Silver Fizz includes the white of one egg, a Golden Fizz uses just the yolk and a Royal Fizz uses the whole egg.

For an example, see:
•*Gin Fizz*
•*Ramos Gin Fizz*

Flip

A flip is an egg-based drink made by combining a spirit and/or wine with a sweetening ingredient and a whole egg. The ingredients are shaken with ice or rolled back and forth between two glasses before they're strained into a wine glass and garnished with nutmeg.

For an example, see:
•*Coffee Cocktail*
•*Gin Flip*

Frappé

This is a style of drink you don't often see today. A Frappé generally indicates an unadorned cordial, but it can refer to a mixed drink as well. The drink is poured into a glass filled with finely crushed ice and then stirred until a frosty sheet of ice forms on the outside of the glass. Sometimes it's strained into a second glass while the ice is emptied from the first glass before pouring the drink back into the first (ice-frosted) glass.

For an example, see:
•*Frappéed Café Royal*

•Mint Julep (which is properly served in the style of a Frappé)

Highball

Originally a Highball was simply Scotch whisky and club soda in a glass with ice. Over time it has come to include any drink made from a spirit and a carbonated beverage. It's one of the simplest and most straightforward drinks around.

For an example, see:
•Cuba Libre
•Dark 'n Stormy
•Moscow Mule
•Pimm's Cup

1940s cocktail menu

Julep

The julep has gone through a variety of transformations over the centuries. Originally the term referred to a strictly medicinal potion, but in the American South it was used to describe a heavily iced beverage combining sugar and mint to a spirit. Just as a cocktail can be described as a "bittered sling," a julep can be described as a "minted sling."

For an example, see:
•Mint Julep

Mist

Similar to a Frappé in that it's served over finely crushed ice, a Mist is almost always a single spirit or liqueur poured over the ice with no attempt at frosting the glass. A Scotch Mist would be the same thing as Scotch on the Rocks except crushed ice is used instead of ice cubes. You rarely see drinks served this way today.

Mull

We've all heard of mulled wine. While there are a variety of different recipes used around the world, they basically all revolve around the addition of spices and sweeteners to a wine before heating the mixture up. Some historical recipes may also include eggs.

Neat

This really isn't a mixed drink style but a way of serving spirits or cordials. To serve a drink "neat" means the requested product is simply poured into a glass without any ice or mixing. Sometimes, a splash of water is added to the spirit, but only at the customer's request.

Negus

The negus is similar to a mull. The main difference is that it is heated through the addition of hot water instead of heating up the wine. Boil water with sugar, citrus, and spices, and then pour this into a pre-heated mug along with some wine or port.

On The Rocks

This refers to a drink served over ice, usually in a rocks (Old Fashioned) glass. The drink can be a single spirit or a standard mixed drink. Customers will often ask for a particular mixed drink or cocktail "on the rocks" if this isn't a traditional way to serve it. For example, a Manhattan is normally served "up" (without ice), but if you'd prefer it on ice, you would order it "on the rocks."

Posset

A Posset is a milk-based hot drink that sometimes includes eggs. It's often made by heating an ale or wine along with some milk, sugar and spices. Whipped eggs are stirred in just before serving.

If you were to heat up a milk punch or an eggnog, you would have a form of Posset.

Punch

The word is thought to have come from the Hindi word *panch*, which means five. With this is mind, it is no surprise that classical punch is made from the combination of five ingredients: spirit, citrus, sugar, spice and water. Originally punch served groups from a large bowl. Over time it worked its way to single serving recipes. In many ways, the more modern exotic drinks of the Tiki Bar era were simply single serving punches.

> *For an example, see:*
> *•Fish House Punch*
> *•Picon Punch*
> *•Planters Punch*

Rickey

The main difference between a Collins and Rickey is that a Rickey is always made with lime juice instead of lemon. The ingredients--a spirit, sweetener and lime juice--are stirred and then emptied into an ice-filled glass and topped with club soda.

For an example, see:
•*Gin Rickey*

Sangaree

A wine punch from the Spanish word "sangria." Traditionally, sangria is made in large batches while a sangaree is a made in single serving sizes. Sangaree mixes wine with a sweetener and sometimes a little citrus. It's served with ice and a sprinkling of nutmeg. It can also be made using ales, spirits or fortified wines like port or madera.

Shot

This can refer either to a single spirit or cordial poured into a shot glass or to what otherwise might be a mixed drink served in a shot glass. The intent is to toss the drink down in one mouthful rather than savoring its flavor.

Shrub

Unlike most drinks which are mixed up relatively quickly, the shrub takes a few days or longer. Usually made by combining fruits, citrus and sugar with boiling water (and/or sometimes vinegar) and a spirit, and then left to sit in an airtight container for several days before straining and bottling.

For an example, see:
•*Brandy Shrub*

Sling

Rarely available today, the sling could be viewed as the precursor to the cocktail. To provide an appropriate context for the consumer of its day, the original definition for the cocktail was a "bittered sling." The sling is made with any spirit combined with a sweetening ingredient and water. Similar to the toddy, the sling, however, uses cold water and/or ice to make it a cold drink instead of a warm one.

For an example, see:
•*Gin Sling*
•*Singapore Sling (a traditional sling that has gotten out of control)*

Smash

As we've noted, Jerry Thomas described the smash as a "julep on a small plan," and such it is. While a julep is usually a large drink savored lovingly while sipped through straws, a smash is prepared quickly, served in a smaller glass and consumed as a common mixed drink. The ingredients are crushed mint, a sweetener and some spirit. The mixture is shaken with ice and then strained as it's poured into an ice-filled glass.

For an example, see:
•*Brandy Smash*

Mint leaf

Sour

You can almost perceive the sour as a simplification of a punch. It represents a fairly important category of mixed drink. It's embodied not only in the Whiskey Sour but also in the Margarita and even the Cosmopolitan. At its core is a careful balance of a sweetener and a sour ingredient like lemon or lime juice. This is combined with the base spirit and then mixed with ice.

For an example, see:
•*Daiquiri*
•*Sidecar*
•*Whiskey Sour*

Swizzle

The Swizzle takes its name from the slightly unique manner in which it's made. A specially made swizzle stick, which has prongs radiating from its base, is spun between the palms to froth or *swizzle* the spirit, citrus juice and sweetener that is in the ice-filled glass or pitcher.

For an example, see:
•*Bermuda Rum Swizzle*

Toddy

A Toddy is almost always a hot drink. If it were made cold, it would be hard to distinguish from a Sling. Traditional recipes consist of a spirit mixed with hot water and a sweetener. It may be garnished with a lemon twist or wedge and a sprinkling of nutmeg or cinnamon.

For an example, see:
•*Hot Toddy*

Up

When a drink is served in a cocktail (martini) glass, without any ice, it is referred to as being served *up*.

Well Drink

More a qualification than a category, *well drinks* are generally encountered on drink menus with perhaps an indication that all *well drinks* are a dollar off during happy hour. The *well* indicates the bargain brand spirits used when the consumer doesn't specifically name the brand of spirit desired. A *well drink* would simply be a drink consisting of one of the well spirits and a mixer. Gin & Tonic would be a well drink, but Tanqueray & Tonic would not.

Bartenders

Bartenders are culinary alchemists using the various liquids and flavorings at hand to create tasty beverages that will entice and entertain their customers' palates with a balance and explosion of flavors reflecting long years of training and carefully honed skills.

Unfortunately, comparing modern American bartenders to the classic bartenders of just a hundred years ago is often like comparing the fry cook at a 24-hour truck stop to a classically trained chef at a celebrated restaurant.

Bartender training used to be long and involved. Its methodology was comparable to that used to train gourmet chefs. However, most bartenders today have no training at all. They tend to rely on a dog-eared recipe book to learn their craft in a trial by fire.

Of course, bartenders make the drinks their customers order. They are rarely challenged. There is, however, a light at the end of the tunnel. An increased understanding of the cocktail is beginning to take place and, with this understanding, consumers are seeking to find bartenders who can realize the culinary potentials of the drinks they make.

Cocktail as Cuisine

The cocktail can and should be seen as a cuisine with all the potential and wonder that this implies.

Circa 1900 Angostura bitters booklet

1950s

Bartenders are masters of this cuisine and should be expected to take their role as seriously as if they were a chef turning out masterful dishes for their customers. Likewise a consumer should approach a cocktail with as much attention to its quality as possible.

Wine, beer and even coffee can be seen as liquid cuisines which embody the notion of craftsmanship, dedication and quality. Like the cocktail, they haven't, however, always been seen as such.

Today, sommeliers are commonplace at restaurants. They help diners create a memorable pairing between the food from the kitchen and the wine from the restaurant's cellar. Drinkers, who would have once seen an inexpensive white zinfandel as their go-to wine, now cherish the robust and complex flavors of a cabernet sauvignon or pinot noir.

Across the nation small microbreweries are producing a variety of craft beers full of flavor and character. While the large commercial breweries and their almost flavorless beers are still top sellers, an educated beer drinker is always on the lookout for new and interesting brews to provide their palate with a little adventure.

Once it was believed that great coffee came out of a can and the percolator was the most popular way to brew a cup. Today, there are a variety of gourmet roasters which have created a dedicated consumer base. People may

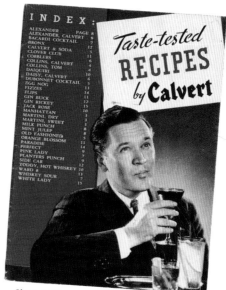

Circa 1950

drive miles out of their way to buy coffee. They will grind whole beans at home and carefully brew their coffee to get just the right flavor for their morning cup.

While cocktails haven't yet achieved this level of large scale craftsmanship, dedication and awareness, there is a definite momentum in that direction. Bartenders are enthusiastically studying, researching and training in order to create exquisite cocktails based on classic methods. Customers are seeking out these bartenders and allowing them to provide drink recommendations instead of simply having the same tried-and-true cocktails over and over again.

The "Cocktailian" Palate

The delight that comes with an appreciation for cocktails is easily acquired. It's a matter of simply educating your palate, not much more difficult but a lot more fun than A-B-C.

The appreciation for unknown flavors is something that we can be open to throughout our lives. There's always a thrill encountering and discovering something new. When we're young and first begin to drink wine, we are unlikely to start with an appreciation of a robust wine like a cabernet sauvignon or zinfandel. Often our choice is a mild sweet wine and the memories of fruit juices and soda pops it produces.

After hiding away in the sweet soda pop wines for a while, we might strive, for example, to impress a date by taking advantage of a sommelier who, by offering an education on the available wines, helps to push our palates forward. Eventually we end up ordering and appreciating the same complex red wines that once sent us running for cover.

Regrettably, there isn't yet the cocktail equivalent of a sommelier, a role model to help our understanding of the culinary potential cocktails can provide. This is why many drinks are closer in a flavor profile to soda pop wines than vintage cabernets.

Balancing Act

Appreciation of the cocktail as a culinary beverage begins with its balance of flavors.

Not too sweet, not too sour, not too strong, but something blending all of the presented flavors in a form that creates what could almost be considered a brand new flavor. This "new" flavor should, as you come to the end of your cocktail, bring a wish that the glass contained a little bit more.

For both the bartender and the consumer, the cocktail should represent a great culinary adventure. This recognition and appreciation will return the dignity and stature the cocktail enjoyed nearly a hundred years ago.

Jigger

The Home Bartender

Unlike beverages such as wine and beer, the making of a cocktail involves an active participation. Anybody can select a great wine. Your chances are good even if you randomly pick a bottle for the sole reason that it has a pretty label on it. But a great cocktail can't get into a glass by accident. It takes a certain amount of skill to know how to properly select and combine the right ingredients, and it takes familiarity and awareness to know a truly good thing when you taste it.

Learning how to make great cocktails can be an exceedingly rewarding experience. It can be learned quickly and then savored lovingly as you expend the time necessary to master it.

As you become more and more secure with the cocktails you make at home, you will discover that you'll be able to make far better choices, with

knowledge and conviction, when you order cocktails and other mixed drinks at the restaurants and cocktail lounges you might visit.

Making cocktails at home can be a relaxing and decompressing ritual after a long day. It takes a short amount of time to gather your bar equipment, the necessary ingredients and artfully prepare a drink for the evening. The process can provide you with a great opportunity to leave behind all of the pressures of the day. The cocktail itself simply becomes the period at the end of the sentence.

During Prohibition, when bars were illegal, it was relatively common for people to have little clandestine cocktail gatherings in their homes. Once Prohibition was lifted, these cocktail parties were held openly, and the cocktail hour was born. During those days, there was little attention paid to cocktail craftsmanship. All

1931

The Tele-Bar was a combination of a 21-inch television, radio, phonograph, and complete bar. 1951.

that seemed to be required were the appropriate accoutrements to make it look like you knew what you were doing. Essentially everybody was happy to have drinking legalized again, so it didn't seem to matter what the drink tasted like. If we remember that the drinks during Prohibition were pretty bad, we can imagine that it didn't take much to seem like an improvement.

Today however we are blessed with wonderful products to choose from, as well as a fairly well-educated population when it comes to understanding and appreciating

quality cuisine. This cultural awareness makes it easier to appreciate the simplicity and enjoyment of making great cocktails at home.

We're now ready to look at the various tools, methods and secrets to making great cocktails at home. We'll see that no shortcuts are necessary and that the home bartender can be as professional as the one at your favorite drinking establishment. We'll discover not only the proper way to make many of the world's most famous cocktails, but why they should be made in a particular way and how it makes a difference.

Viva la Cocktail!

Most of the drinks that follow can be prepared without any specific cocktail making tools. There are only a few things truly necessary for creating great cocktails.

Tools of the Trade

If you are currently without tools and plan a shopping trip using the advice below, I would like to caution against spending too much money on any of these tools. Your skill improves as you use a tool and gain a better understanding of it. If you then feel that you could have made a better choice, you will be able to make a more enlightened selection based on what you've learned. So, don't spend a lot. Simply assume that your first purchase is likely to be experimental and that your second purchase will be made with a better understanding of what you really need.

Measuring

Cocktail recipes may call for as little as $\frac{1}{4}$ ounce (7ml) or even a dash for certain ingredients. When measuring small amounts, especially ones with as much flavor as lemon juice, it's crucial to get an accurate measurement. This could be the difference between a great cocktail and a terrible one. Sure, you may see bartenders pouring products straight from bottles into mixing glasses without seeming to measure

them. Trust me, it's not as easy as the bartender makes it appear.

Knowing the proper translations between ounces and teaspoons will allow you to use whatever measuring spoons you have on hand. Further, if you can look at a recipe and understand the ratios of the ingredients being used, you can even use the cap from your bottle of gin to make a drink. Two capfuls of this, three capfuls of that and six capfuls of gin. A lot of measuring is simply understanding ratios. If you do, you can size up or down any cocktail recipe you encounter.

Mixing

Most, but not all, mixed drinks are made in a vessel separate from the glass they are served in. Sometimes they are stirred, sometimes they are shaken. One important concept in making a great cocktail is knowing when to shake and when to stir. An old peanut butter jar properly cleaned can easily be used for either task.

If a cocktail is to be shaken, just screw the lid on and shake away (but perhaps not too hard). If the cocktail is to be stirred, any old mixing implement that works well with ice, can do the trick. An old chopstick, perhaps?

Chilling

An often misunderstood component of mixed drinks is the ice used for chilling. It's very important to have

plenty of ice on hand, and fresh ice is always preferred to ice that has been sitting in the icebox too long gathering flavors from last week's frozen stroganoff. Sometimes freezing fresh ice and throwing it into a zip-top freezer bag is all it takes to make sure you have an ample supply that isn't getting exposed to freezer funk.

Straining

It's important to have something handy to strain ice and whatever else might be in your mixing glass from what you actually want in the drink you serve. In a pinch, almost anything will do, even a slotted spoon.

Serving

If you are serving guests you want to impress, you may want to make sure you have reasonably nice glasses in which to serve the drinks. This would probably not be the time to bring out the old Flintstone jam jars to serve a Manhattan. However, if you're making drinks just for you and a close and understanding friend, anything goes.

That's really it! The basic tools you'll need for making a great cocktail. Of course, there are a number of items you may decide are worth having if, for no other reason, than to make the job easier. You could look at these as "extra credit" tools. Let's take a quick look at the possibilities.

The Basic Kit

For your bare bones bartending kit, you should pick up the following:

- •Jigger
- •Cocktail Shaker
- •Bar Spoon
- •Strainer
- •Cocktail Glasses

Jigger

A jigger is a small measuring glass and possibly the most problematic tool. The jiggers generally found in kitchen stores rarely tell you how many ounces they are measuring. This is an obvious problem. Also, their shape is usually conical. This might not pose a problem when you need a full measure, but what if your jigger measures 1 ounce (30ml) and you need $\frac{3}{4}$ (22ml)? Conical shapes are terrible for eyeballing a partial measure accurately. The best cocktail measures are the ones that clearly and accurately provide measures for up to two ounces in $\frac{1}{4}$ ounce (7ml) increments.

Although I usually don't like getting brand specific on products of this nature, I will say that my personal favorite jigger for home use is the OXO Mini Angled Measure. Generally you'll find it with the measuring cups at your local kitchen store rather than the bar tools section.

Cocktail Shaker

This can be another slightly problematic purchase. There are essentially two types of cocktail shakers. The most common is the Combination, sometimes referred to as a Cobbler style shaker. They are also known as Three Part because they consist of three separate parts. The lower part is the mixing tin, the middle part is the cover with an integrated strainer and the third is the cap, which tightly covers the strainer so you can shake up a drink without spilling things. Personally I don't recommend this style of shaker. You'll find that most bars don't use this style either. They don't work effectively, and the middle portion often sticks to the bottom.

The second style is what is commonly known as a Boston Shaker. This

Jiggers

Boston Shaker

Parisian Shaker

Three Part Shaker

consists of a pint glass (a.k.a. mixing glass) and a metal mixing tin. The mixing tin is larger than the pint glass, allowing one to fit tightly within the other. When the shaker is properly sealed, you can quickly and easily shake up any cocktail. You should note that it often takes a little time to gain the experience to properly seal the shaker. Warning: When it isn't properly sealed, you end up with the drink all over yourself, or worse yet, your guests.

A variation of the Boston Shaker is a two part metal shaker with an elegant curve on the top. These are often referred to as Parisian shakers since they were popularized by bartenders in Paris.

My personal recommendation is for the Boston Shaker style. Most of the best bartenders use this and, with just a little practice, it's quite effective.

A few tips for properly using a Boston Shaker: first, measure the liquid ingredients into the pint glass. Put the ice into the metal mixing tin. Then pour the contents of the pint glass into the mixing tin and solidly place the inverted mixing glass over and into the mixing tin. Give the bottom of the glass a solid whack with your palm to seal the two together. Holding the mixing tin tightly in your left hand and the mixing glass in your right hand, solidly shake the drink.

When you're finished shaking, hold the mixing tin in your left hand. With the palm of your right hand, give a solid whack to the side of the mixing tin where you imagine the edge of the mixing glass to be. This will almost always separate the two so you can easily strain the drink. It does, however, take a little practice.

Bar Spoon

Since not all drinks need to be shaken (another a good reason to use a Boston Shaker), this is a good time to ask

"when do I shake?" and "when do I stir?" There's a secret to the answer which few modern bartenders seem to know.

The purpose of shaking or stirring is to chill the drink as well as provide some dilution of the ice into the drink (which is important!). Both shaking and stirring do an equal job of this. Stirring takes a little longer, however, but shaking dilutes the drink more. In the end, it's all pretty much a wash. The reason you want to stir a drink is to prevent the shaking from clouding and/or foaming up the drink. It's all about presentation. You'll want to stir a drink with all clear ingredients (like a Martini or Manhattan) so when it's poured into the cocktail glass, it will come out perfectly clear. If the drink has any cloudy or opaque ingredients (like lemon juice, milk, cream, etc.), it might as well be shaken, since it won't end up clear no matter what you do.

This means you'll need a bar spoon for stirring. Currently in America, we don't have much of a choice. The common bar spoon is a cheap metal spoon with an overly large bowl and a plastic red knob on the end. However, Europeans will find a variety of spoons. Many of them are quite solid with a nice heavy tamping end on them.

Bar spoons

INTRODUCTION

Strainer

Once you've stirred or shaken your drink properly, the next step is often to strain it into the glass. The common strainer here is the Hawthorne Strainer (also spelled "Hawthorn," however the historically accurate spelling includes the final "e"). This is a slightly funny looking strainer with a spring around the edge of it. This type of strainer fits really well in the mixing tin of the Boston Shaker, and it is a little tight in the pint glass.

A good Hawthorne Strainer is probably all you need, but you might also want to consider a Julep Strainer. These are harder to find, but they fit nicely within the mixing glass portion of the Boston Shaker and work best when you stir a cocktail instead of shake it.

Hawthorne Strainer

Julep Strainer

Glassware

After taking the time and care to mix your drink properly, you probably want to attractively present it in the proper glassware. Some people get very particular about their glassware and insist that *this* drink should always be served in *that* glass. In truth it really doesn't matter that much. While the recent trend has been to carefully match a particular wine with a particular glass that best accentuates its flavors, mixed drinks may be served in any appropriately-sized glass you want to use.

I frankly recommend that you try to have a little fun with your glassware

choices. Check out antique shops where you'll find various shapes and sizes of glasses and mix things up a little.

Look through a glassware catalog and you'll find over a dozen types of glasses. However, these are easily divided up into three different categories: stemware, tumblers and mugs.

Let's take a look at some of the more common types of glasses in each of these categories. Later, in the recipe section, you will see the associated icon for a particular glass listed next to the recipe. This indicates which glass is appropriate for that drink.

1950s placemat

Stemware

As the name implies, this is a glass with a stem of some sort. A glass with a short stem is often referred to as a footed glass.

Types of stemware include:

 ## Wine

A typical wineglass is a bulbous glass that slightly narrows at the top to help hold aromas. Small wineglasses with fancy etchings can be fun to use for all sorts of drinks.

 ## Cocktail (a.k.a. martini)

Cocktails were originally served in small, fancy wine glasses. According to cocktail lore, the common V-shaped glass was popularized at the 1925 Paris Exposition.

The drink most commonly associated with this glass is the Martini. In fact, this association between drink and glass is so strong that many people consider any drink served this way is a Martini, which of course it isn't.

Originally cocktail glasses were around four ounces in size, but over time the tendency to think bigger means better made it hard to find a glass less than nine ounces. Frankly, that is far too large for a sensible drink. If possible, I recommend trying to find a glass closer to six ounces (or even less) in size. There's a lot of fun to be had scouring antique stores looking for old cocktail glasses or even champagne coupes, which work quite nicely.

 ## Champagne coupe (a.k.a. saucer)

Looking like a cocktail glass with voluptuous curves, this was once the preferred glass for serving champagne. Often it would have a hollow stem from which a beautiful tower of bubbles emerged. Today the flute glass has replaced the coupe as the glassware of choice for champagne and the coupe is used as a fancy replacement for the cocktail glass. Feel free to use a champagne coupe, which is elegant and reasonably sized, for any drink that might otherwise be served in a V-shaped glass.

 ## Champagne flute (a.k.a. tulip)

This tall and narrow stemmed glass has replaced the coupe as the preferred glass to serve sparkling wine. It provides a beautiful display of bubbles and, because it has less exposed surface area, it keeps the carbonation a bit longer.

It can often be fun to serve sour style cocktails (sidecar, daiquiri, cosmopolitan, etc.) in a flute glass.

Tumblers

A tumbler is any glass without a stem, foot, handle or other such adornment. Usually, but not always, tumblers have straight vertical sides.

Types of tumblers include:

 ### Rocks (a.k.a. lowball, Old Fashioned, bucket)

Short and squat, usually about as high as it is wide, this glass is commonly used for simple drinks served with ice. Normally close to 8 ounces (240ml) in size, you would use this for a Scotch on the Rocks, Old Fashioned or a Gin & Tonic.

 ### Delmonico (a.k.a. fizz, rickey, juice glass)

Rarely referred to these days as a Delmonico glass, these are slightly smaller glasses. They are typically a little taller and narrower than a rocks glass, about 5 ounces (150ml) in size with straight sides.

 ### Highball

Similar to the Delmonico, but taller and wider. Usually holding from 8 to 10 ounces (240 to 360ml), this glass is commonly used for… well… highballs, or drinks which combine a spirit, mixer and ice. In a typical restaurant, this might be the glass used to serve iced water.

 ### Collins (a.k.a. chimney)

Along the same lines as the Delmonico and highball, this glass is taller than a highball and about as wide as a Delmonico. It usually holds from 10 to 12 ounces (360 to 420ml), and would be used for, of course, a Collins, but also for a variety of thirst-quenching summer drinks. These glasses will sometimes have a frosted exterior intended to accentuate the concept of *cold and refreshing*.

 ### Mugs

As you might expect, a mug is virtually any glass with a handle of some sort. While the glasses listed here are usually (but not always) made from clear glass, mugs are made from a variety of materials: glass, ceramic, metal, wood, etc.

The handle is typically intended to make it easier to drink hot beverages, and so most hot drinks will be served in a mug. There are, however, notable exceptions, such as punch and the Moscow Mule in its iconic copper mug.

1947

Extra Credit

Although we've covered most of what you need to make great cocktails at home, there are a few other tools which might be handy as your skills evolve.

Channel Knife

One of the more common types of cocktail garnish is a lemon twist. The channel knife is a special tool specifically designed to cut those simple little spirals.

To cut a well formed spiral, it's best to use fresh fruit. No matter if it's a lemon, orange, lime or any other citrus you might want to try, spiraling always works best when the fruit is fresh and the skin is nice and tight. Also, always cut the spiral over the drink you'll be serving. As you're cutting a spiral twist, oils from the skin of the citrus will be expelled in a flavorful mist and by cutting over the drink, you'll be making the most use of this flavor.

Vegetable Peeler

A channel knife can cut a very narrow twist, but sometimes you want something a little more substantial. A common vegetable peeler can easily cut a nice solid plank out of most citrus fruits. Remember to cut the twist over the drink. To provide the best possible visual appeal, square the edges of the peel by carefully cleaning it with a knife.

Juicer

Many cocktails contain citrus juice. Try to avoid pre-made or commercial juice. Freshly squeezed juices always insure a better drink. If, because of time constraints, you have to squeeze

Juicers

juice ahead of time, try not to let it sit too long. If the juice sits longer than a few hours, it will start to get bitter instead of sour.

There are a wide variety of juicers available. The best ones for cocktails will be those that will expel some of the essential oils from the skin of the fruit into the juice. Mexican Juicers do a good job of this because they essentially turn the fruit inside out as they squeeze out its juices. Their downside is that they're a little messy.

Muddler

The traditional muddler often looks like a miniature baseball bat. It's used much the same way a mortar and pestle are. The muddler is the pestle and the mixing glass is the mortar.

You can use a muddler for crushing sugar cubes, rendering juice from a quartered lime or crushing mint leaves and other herbs to extract their essences. Remember, you shouldn't be too aggressive, especially when herbs are involved. If you grind mint leaves too much, you'll start to extract some of the bitter enzymes they contain instead of just the fresh mint flavor.

Also, be careful of the Seattle Muddle, which is dropping some citrus wedges in a glass, topping it with ice, then muddling through the ice with the mistaken impression that you are getting some great juice. Instead, you are fighting through the ice and barely touching the wedges. A better technique is to dry muddle

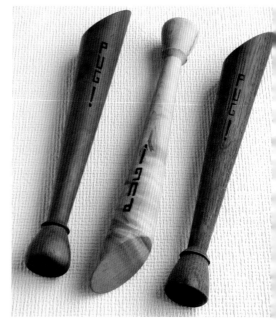

Muddlers

(muddle without ice) or, better yet, muddle with a little granulated sugar if the recipe calls for it. The sugar will abrade the skin of the citrus and extract more of its oils.

Knife

From slicing citrus to cutting the foils off wine bottles, good knives will have multiple uses behind the bar.

It's usually best to have a couple different sizes. While a paring knife will satisfy most of your needs, a chef's knife, for example, is better for cutting larger fruit.

Come to think of it, a cutting board wouldn't be a bad idea either.

Cocktail Pitcher

As previously mentioned, not all cocktails are shaken. While you can use the mixing glass portion of a Boston Shaker for stirring your cocktails, I personally prefer a cocktail pitcher for this. Today, most are made of glass and come with a handle and a formed spout. The spout should be designed to automatically hold back the ice or you'll need to use your hawthorn or julep strainer to help hold back the ice as you pour.

My favorite cocktail pitchers have a metal rim around the top with a built-in strainer. To the best of my knowledge, nobody is making these anymore. Look for them in antique shops or online auctions.

Mesh Strainer

A mesh strainer is used to *double-strain* a drink. We may be getting a little fussy here, but many bars will choose to fine strain some cocktails to keep any pulp or ice shards from getting into the glasses. For most purposes, a small fine hand-strainer will do the job nicely.

Soda Siphon

Bottled soda is both common and cheap these days, but this was not always the case. Not too far in the distant past, fresh pressurized soda

bottles were delivered to restaurants, bars and even homes. Today, if you wish to serve soda from a soda siphon, you can easily pick up your own CO_2 cartridges and pressurize the soda yourself.

The use of a soda siphon gives you a bit of retro flair, and it can be fun as well. You can even make your own soda flavors by adding a splash of syrup or other flavoring to the glass before adding the soda.

Ice Cracker

Ice, as we've mentioned, is an important component when you make a drink. You want ice that is large enough to bring a good strong chill to the drink yet small enough to move well when you stir or shake it.

When you serve a drink on the rocks, you'll find that well-proportioned ice not only looks good in the glass, it maintains a fine chill as it melts and gradually adds additional water to the drink.

Since it's easier to turn big ice into small ice, it's best to start off with ice cubes that are large and roughly square in shape. If you find that the ice is larger then desired, you'll need to break it up. A solid whack with the back of your bar spoon or muddler will service well for this, but you may also consider a special ice cracker specifically designed to crack ice neatly and effectively.

Lewis Bag

At times you'll need not just small ice, but really, really small ice. A Mojito is traditionally made with ice crushed to the size of small kernels of corn, and a Mint Julep should be made with ice that's almost powdered.

You can buy special ice crushing machines to handle this task, but a simple, effective and inexpensive tool for doing this is a Lewis Bag. Essentially this is just a canvas bag you put the ice into and then pound with your muddler or rubber/wooden mallet until you get it to the size you need. The canvas will absorb any melted water, leaving the ice nice and dry.

Double-straining

Stocking Your Home Bar

If you're interested in setting up a home bar, you've probably seen, if not looked for, a comprehensive shopping list of the general purpose spirits, cordials, mixers and flavorings that you'll need to make many of the drinks in this or any other cocktail recipe book.

Frankly, this approach is fraught with problems. For one thing, it can be very expensive, and the cost may drive you to settle for cheaper and often inferior products. For another thing, you can end up with lots of products you never actually use.

Fortunately, there's an excellent solution to these problems.

Rather than starting with a shopping list of products to buy, why not select a cocktail you want to make. Look up the recipe for that cocktail, and pick up just the products you need for that one drink. Simple, straightforward and effective.

For the next week or so, make that drink over and over again. Reach a point where you really understand what each ingredient is doing to the drink, and how the way you prepare it comes into play. Play around with the recipe a little bit. Perhaps look up a few alternate recipes and see how the drink is changed.

In effect, you want to *own* this drink. You want to fully understand what defines the drink and allows it to strut its stuff. Then, select another drink and start the whole process all over again.

Eventually, you will start to run out of one product or another. Before you reach empty, go buy a replacement, but whatever you do, don't buy the same brand. By selecting another brand, you can do a taste test to determine your preference. In this way you will discover the products you personally like best for the cocktails you make the most.

There are multiple benefits from this approach. First, you're going to spend a lot less on your first liquor store run. Second, you're going to have a tighter focus on what you're trying to achieve. Third, after a couple of months, you're going to have a well stocked liquor cabinet. And finally, you're going to know how to make a great cocktail with every single product in your cabinet.

The Cocktail Party

Eventually, you're going to want to throw a cocktail party.

The most important thing to remember is that you don't need to be prepared to make every cocktail under the sun. Just like you plan the menu for a dinner party, you need to plan the menu for a cocktail party.

You should select two, three or, at the very most, four different cocktails that you think will be appropriate for your guests. You'll also have some beer and wine available for those who don't think they're into cocktails, as well as some non-alcoholic alternatives for those who prefer not to drink.

If it's a really small party, you may choose to make the drinks yourself. In that case you won't ask people what they want, but instead mix a pitcher or tray full of the cocktail you want to serve and distribute that to the guests. Think of your cocktail choices as different courses proceeding in a pre-selected order.

If the party is larger, you can set up a self-host bar with all the necessary ingredients to make the specific drinks you've selected. You'll want to prepare recipe sheets that provide clear instructions on making each of the selected drinks. This means, of course, you'll want to select drinks that can be made easily with little intervention. You may want to hover around the bar periodically to help your guests feel comfortable with making their own drinks.

For really large parties, there's really only one way to make certain everybody is comfortable and happy and that you aren't spending your entire time troubleshooting issues. You'll need to hire somebody to tend bar for you.

When considering how many cocktails to prepare, the best rule of thumb is to plan on three drinks per person, and that each (750 ml) bottle of spirits will make a little more than 15 cocktails.

So, if you're going to make just Daiquiris all night long and you have 10 people attending, you'll need at least two bottles of rum.

Holding parties is always a learning experience. To build your confidence in both cocktail preparation and party planning, begin with smaller parties with close friends. Gradually build to something larger. Perhaps plan your first couple parties as dinner parties in which one specific cocktail is served to everybody as an *apéritif* before the meal starts. You can share a little bit about the cocktail and how it's made with your guests. In this way, you will make the evening far easier on yourself. You'll be able, too, to share some of your passion about the cocktails you are making for them.

Mixology 101

We've now covered a lot of the basic material and it's time to look at some of the terminology, techniques and secrets that every good bartender should know. Some of these will simply add to your knowledge, but many will allow you to make far better cocktails than you might otherwise.

Balance

To me, the most essential secret to great cocktails involves balance. Any drink served should strike a careful balance among all the flavors contained. It shouldn't taste boozy, nor should it be watery. Sweet ingredients shouldn't overwhelm everything else. Likewise, a drink that's too sour will be sipped and quickly put down. Strive to make the entire drink enchanting and tasteful, all the way to the last sip.

Ingredients

Use quality ingredients if you want to make a quality cocktail. Keep comparing different products to discover which ingredients work best for the drinks you are making. For a less expensive way to compare spirits, look for mini-bottles at your local liquor store.

Measuring

Often you'll see bartenders pour ingredients without seeming to measure. In fact, they have taught themselves to do this and, with practice, they're able to get amazingly close to the correct measurements.

However, when making cocktails, it's essential to measure as accurately as possible. Even when ingredients are measured in increments as small as $1/4$ ounce (7ml), you'll soon realize that the slightest variation will change the flavor of the drink you are making. So take the time to carefully and accurately measure each ingredient you are using.

Ice

It's easy to overlook an ingredient as important as ice, but we shouldn't. Ice plays an extremely important role in any mixed drink. Not only is it providing such a signature component as the chill to the drink, it also is providing an important hidden ingredient in the form of water.

As ice chills, it also melts, and as it melts, it releases water into the drink. Don't assume that water is a bad thing because it will dilute the drink. The amount of alcohol in the drink doesn't decrease as ice melts in the glass. What really happens is the sharp bite of the alcohol gets tamed by the gentle smoothness of water. This is crucial for the balance we are striving for.

Some people will store their alcohol in a freezer to guarantee they can make the coldest drinks possible. Unfortunately, this hurts the overall quality of a drink because ice won't melt as fast in ice cold spirits. Thus, the proper amount of water won't get added, and the drink will end up being overly *hot* with alcohol. If you want a good drink, you should be looking for the balance that the water will add.

So, keep your booze out of the freezer, and keep your ice cold, clean and in good supply.

Shaking versus Stirring

We've established that the purpose of both shaking and stirring is essentially the same, to chill the drink down rapidly and to that end, both do an equally great job of it. There are, however, slight differences between the two. Stirring takes longer to chill the drink than shaking, but, in the end, the same amount of water gets released into the drink. This might make you feel that shaking is the preferred way to mix a cocktail. Shaking, however, will agitate the drink more and infuse it with air bubbles. This will make the drink cloudy, and often leave a less than desirable foam on top. Stirring, on the other hand, will leave the drink almost crystal clear.

So which should you use, and when? There's one basic rule of thumb which we touched upon earlier, but it's worth repeating. If the drink is made from all clear ingredients, it should be stirred in order to preserve the clarity. On the other hand, if the drink includes milk, cream, an opaque or cloudy ingredient or eggs, it should be shaken since nothing you do will make it clear.

Chilled Glassware

Cocktails should be served well chilled. Pouring a cold liquid into a room temperature glass, however, will quickly start warming the drink as the thermal dynamics between the glass and the liquid strive to balance out.

Chilling the glasses first is an important step in making a great cocktail. The easiest way to do this is to store your glasses in the freezer. At home, however, you may not be able to find that much room in your freezer. Many bars, in fact, have dedicated refrigerators specifically for this purpose.

An easy way to chill your glasses at home is to place some cracked ice in the glass and fill the glass with water. Do this before you start making your drink so it has plenty of time to chill. Before pouring your drink into the glass, make sure you pour the melted water out. Be a little sloppy about it. If you allow the chilled water to spread down the outside of the glass, it will help chill that side as well.

Garnishes

Adding a beautiful garnish to a cocktail is the final step in making a great drink. There are a variety of common garnishes. These include citrus twists or wedges, cherries, olives, mint, pineapple, even edible flowers and little paper umbrellas. There really isn't much limiting what you can use for a garnish, but you should always be careful to select garnishes appropriate for the cocktail and/or the situation.

Often a simple twist of lemon peel can be the best and easiest way to garnish a drink. There is, however, a right way

to do this so that it provides the most effective transformation to the drink.

Using a channel knife or vegetable peeler, you want to cut the twist over the drink. This allows oils from the skin to be expelled over the drink and add some additional flavorings to accent the drink. In addition, you may

want to rub the twist around the edge of the glass before dropping it in. This will add additional oils to the glass edge, which will further accentuate the drink with each sip. Be sure to rub the colored side of the peel against the glass and not the pithy white. The flavorful oils lie on the outside peel.

Rimming

Some cocktails will rely on rimming a glass with some sort of flavoring. For a Margarita this is often salt, for a Lemon Drop it is usually sugar and for a Bloody Mary it can be a combination of salt, chili powder and, perhaps, some dried herbs.

You can buy a foam pad to moisten the glass with as well as special containers to hold the sugar and salt. Frankly, these work best in bars where speed is more important than quality.

The best way to rim a glass is to first moisten the rim of the glass with something that will help the rimming spice stick. A quick method is to take

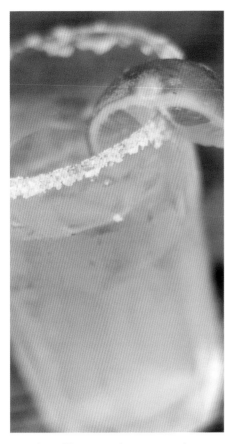

When rimming with sugar, keep in mind that moisture on the outside of the glass will cause the sugar to migrate down the glass, forming a messy sticky film. Sugared rims are best done an hour or so before the glass is to be used, giving the water a chance to dry. This will also harden the sugar into a nice shell and keep your fingers from getting too sticky.

Nothing is written in stone

As you continue to learn about cocktails and mixed drinks, you will encounter recipes that differ or contradict one another. This is natural, and you shouldn't let it confuse you. Just as there are many different ways to make something as common as hash browns, so you'll find different ways have come about to make different drinks. Some recipes and methods are better than others. When you encounter a different approach, take the time to see how it differs from what you're used to and determine for yourself how it might change the drink. You might even experiment a little on your own, and see if you can improve upon some of the recipes and methods found here.

a wedge of lemon or lime, cut a slot in the fruit, and, inserting the rim into the slot, rub it around the edge of the glass. If a rim is to be sugared, you can dip the rim in a little plate of simple syrup.

By putting your rimming material in the outer ring of a tea saucer, you can easily invert the glass into the saucer and the salt, sugar, or spice will stick reasonably well. A better way, however, one which will rim only the outside of the drink, is to use a spoon to cascade the rimming material on the outside of the glass. In this way you can create a nice wide, not to mention very dramatic, rim.

The Base Spirits

What is a Spirit?

At the core of the bartender's stash of ingredients is what is commonly referred to as the base spirits. Simply defined, there are six base spirits: brandy, gin, rum, tequila, vodka and whiskey. Usually, but not always, one of these will be the foundation of any mixed drink or cocktail.

Spirits start with a fermented product which, due to the limitations of yeast, has a low alcohol content, usually around 15% ABV (alcohol by volume). This alcohol is then concentrated through distillation. Distillation is capable of increasing the alcohol content to almost, but not quite, pure alcohol.

As the distillation concentrates the alcohol, the flavors and character of the base fermented product are tuned, enhanced and clarified. Straight corn whiskey fresh from the still will have a wonderful clean flavor of corn. With continued distillation and the accompanying rise of the alcohol level most of the distinctive flavors of the initial product begin to get stripped away. This leaves the crisp burn of the alcohol and some lingering flavor fragments coming from fusel oils and other contaminates that are difficult to strip out completely. A distiller must find the right balance, capturing the desirable flavors while discarding the unwanted flavors and contaminants.

There are various laws governing the alcoholic concentration of spirits in order for a spirit to carry a particular spirit designation. Generally distillers won't approach that level, since so much of the character would be removed that it won't have the sought-after quality. For example, whiskey, depending on classification, can't be distilled above 80% alcohol (160 proof). Most distillers will distill only to 65% alcohol (130 proof). On the other hand, for a spirit to be designated vodka, it is necessary to distill to at least 95% alcohol (190 proof). Most vodka is distilled to a slightly higher proof to remove as much of the character and contaminants from the original fermented product as possible.

You can't get 100% pure alcohol from distillation. Not only are the final contaminants too hard to get out but alcohol is hydroscopic, which means it attracts water. So the only way to get pure alcohol from not-quite-pure alcohol is to apply chemicals to strip out the remaining contaminants and water. The problem with this, however, is that once the pure alcohol is exposed to air, it will begin to draw moister out of the air until it reaches around 97% alcohol.

Once the distillation process is finished several types of spirits are destined to spend time in barrels. The alcohol level plays a roll here as well. Too high an alcohol level will draw unwanted woody flavors from the barrels. If too low, it won't draw the desired flavors from the barrel. Some spirits are distilled to a level considered too high for proper barrel aging, and so water is added to arrive at the right level.

Once in barrels, several changes take place. Most notable is coloring. Going into the barrel all spirits are crystal clear. Coloration comes strictly from the wood aging. Aging also causes the inherent characteristics of the original spirit to mellow and mature while losing their sharp bright edges. As temperature fluctuations cause the spirit to expand into the actual wood of the barrel and back out again, some flavoring is added to the spirit. At the same time, the spirit is also passing through the char layer on the inside of the barrel, providing some level of filtration and purification. The result is a smoother and mellower spirit with some additional complex characteristics. All this is highly desirable in a quality product.

The next step in process is bottling. Here, too, the alcoholic level is important. In America, most spirits are required to be bottled at no less than 40% alcohol (80 proof), and most spirits not bottled at much more than that.

The final stage in the life of a spirit is its use in mixed drinks, and, here as well, the alcohol level plays a role. Consumers rarely know or consider the alcoholic content of the drinks set before them. But when you mix a drink, you want to provide a consistency of potency. If you happen to be using a high proof spirit such as a *Navy Strength* gin (traditionally made to the specifications of the Royal Navy), then you should do so in a smaller glass than you'd serve a normal strength drink. This also means that it wouldn't be a bad idea to serve a Martini, which is made up of all alcoholic ingredients, in a smaller glass or portion than a Sidecar, which includes some citrus juice.

Each of the six recognized base spirits have distinctive characteristics and history. Let's take a look at those differences and examine a little bit of their history and usages in cocktails.

Brandy

Brandy is the classification given to any spirit which is based on fruit. While almost any fruit can be used to make a brandy, grapes are the most common. A bottle simply labeled as brandy is most likely made from a distilled wine. Brandy from other fruits will be labeled as Cherry Brandy, Peach Brandy or whatever is appropriate. There are some fruit brandies which have taken on specific names, such as Calvados for apple brandy made in Normandy, applejack for apple brandy made in America, Kirsch or Kirshwasser for cherry brandy, Slivovitz for plum brandy, etc.

Brandy from fruit other than grapes is also often referred to as *eau de vie*, which translates from the French as *water of life*. An *eau de vie* will almost always be clear since traditionally it's never aged.

HISTORY

In the 1500s the Dutch popularized brandy and gave it its name. They referred to it as *brandewijn*, which means *burnt wine*. The name refers to the distillation process where wine is concentrated through the application of heat. Distilling wine was thought to make it cheaper and easier to ship. Further, a tax loophole provided an added bonus since spirituous beverages of the day were taxed on volume instead of alcohol percentages.

The Germans followed the Dutch closely, and referred to brandy first as *branntwein* and later as *weinbrand*, both of which mean *burnt wine*. The French called it *brandevin*, which the English turned into *brandywine*, later shortened to just *brandy*.

DRINKING BRANDY

When sipped neat, brandy is often served in what is commonly referred to as a balloon snifter, exemplified by an extremely large bowl glass atop a very short foot. The intent of such a glass is to provide a wide surface area which will provide ample room for the aromas to rise from the brandy, which are then concentrated in the narrower opening. The opening should not be too narrow however, or else it focuses too much of the alcohol coming off of the brandy, which will produce a burning sensation in the nose. Likewise it is not recommended to heat your brandy, as is often seen, since this will even further increase the alcohols being vaporized. The flavors of a quality brandy are also enjoyed at room temperature, or slightly below, then they are at higher temperatures.

Cognac and Armagnac

To say that cognac and armagnac are nothing more than brandies is both being truthful and disrespectful at the same time. A brandy can only be labeled cognac or armagnac if it is made in those specific regions of France, following specific methods and processes.

Today, cognac is the more popular of the two, a result of geography more than anything else. The Cognac region of France has an easier access to the sea and therefore distribution than its land-locked cousin does.

VERY SUPERIOR OLD PALE

You will often see labeling such as VS (Very Superior), VSOP (Very Superior Old Pale) and XO (Extra Old) on both armagnac and cognac. This is an attempt to indicate aging and quality in relation to other products

from the same brand. Armagnac and cognac have slight differences in the requirements behind these designations, but essentially VS is a very young brandy, VSOP is slightly older and XO is slightly older than that. It is difficult to make quality judgments between different brands solely on their label designation. A VSOP from one brand can often be better than an XO from another.

POMACE BRANDY

While true brandy is produced from wine, pomace brandy is produced from the leftovers of the winemaking process. This includes the skins, seeds and stems remaining after crushing the grape and filtering off the juice. Originally, these pomace brandies were crudely made, and the result was a rather fiery product. Recently, better craftsmanship has led to a product that is smooth and rich in character.

Pomace brandy is made in several countries around the world, most notably Grappa from Italy, Marc from France, and Pisco from Peru and Chile.

Rum

Rum is a distilled product made from sugar in sugar cane juice, sugar syrup or molasses. The process is relatively simple, even more so than most other spirits, since there isn't any need for special processing to prepare the sugars to feed the yeasts that will in turn produce the alcohol.

Sugar cane

Modern rum production is centered in the Caribbean Islands since they are one of the major producers of sugar cane in the world.

However, sugar cane is not indigenous to the area. It's a plant introduced by Christopher Columbus. Since it quickly proved to be a hearty crop, a lucrative industry was established to satisfy the growing sweet tooth of Europe.

One by-product of refining sugar is molasses. Initially, molasses was seen as a waste product, but soon somebody had the idea of fermenting the molasses to see what could be made from it. This was the beginning of rum.

Early rums were unsophisticated, almost undrinkable. If it weren't for the fact that the initial customers for rum were sailors putting into port after many months at sea who were more than willing to drink almost anything, rum production might never have had a phase two.

Over time, an evolution took place in the distillation and aging processes, allowing the quality of rum to steadily

increase.

During the early colonial days, both France and England were concerned that this imported spirit would hurt local sales of their gins and brandies. They quickly passed import laws making it expensive, if not impossible, to bring rum to Europe. America had no such concerns, and soon rum became the favored spirit. George Washington even imported rum to be served at his inauguration.

Later, American whiskey would take center stage in the New World, and the use of rum became less common. It wouldn't be until Prohibition that rum would once again become an important

INTRODUCTION

American spirit. And, as we've seen, after Prohibition, through the creative talents of Don the Beachcomber and Trader Vic, America would be re-introduced to rum on a grand scale through exotic drinks almost entirely reliant on rum as a base spirit.

RHUM AGRICOLE

While normal rum is made from what could be referred to as the industrial waste of the sugar refining process, there is another type of rum called *rhum agricole* which is made from juices extracted directly from the sugar cane itself.

CACHAÇA

Brazil has a huge sugar cane industry, and, as you might expect, they also have a big industry producing spirits from the sugar cane. Early cachaça was no doubt a low quality product equal to the early rums. Recently, however, cachaça production has improved immensely as has its popularity. There are now many very fine cachaças available, but, unfortunately, they are rarely exported.

Whiskey

Simply put, whiskey is a product distilled from grain. Just as you can consider brandy as being distilled from wine, you can consider whiskey as being distilled from beer, although a beer to which hops haven't been added.

Whiskey gets its name from *uisgebeatha* (Irish) and *uisgebaugh* (Scottish), both of which translate as *water of life*. The names, being somewhat difficult for non-native speakers to pronounce, were eventually simplified to *whiskey*.

TO *E* OR NOT TO *E*

The landscapes of whiskies are quite complex and for those seeking complexity, look no further than its spelling.

You will see whiskey spelt both as *whiskey* and *whisky*. Traditionally you use *whiskey* when you refer to Irish or American whiskey. And you use *whisky* when you refer to Scotch or Canadian whisky. Precisely why this came about is debatable, and it isn't without its exceptions. Here in America, both Maker's Mark and George Dickle label their products as *whisky*.

MALTING

Whiskey making begins with the creation of a fermented product made from whichever grain you choose to use. Since the sugars in grain are

Barley

locked up tight in its starch layer and unavailable to the yeast in this form, the fermentation is accomplished by allowing the grain to germinate (sprout). This releases an enzyme converting the starches trapped in the grain to sugars. These sugars then feed the growing plant. But, what we really want is for these sugars to feed the yeasts to produce alcohol, so we must stop the germination process before it goes too far. This is done by applying heat to the grain.

The process of applying heat to the grain is called malting and is important for the production of both beer and whiskey. All whiskies start with the malting process, but then differences in production allow each to have their own unique characteristics.

BLENDED WHISKIES

As the name implies, this is a whiskey made from a blending of different whiskies. Typically, it's not only a blend from multiple distillers, but it's also a blend of true whiskey and a grain whiskey distilled so high that most, if not all, of its distinctive characteristics are removed. This is often referred to as a neutral grain spirit.

IRISH WHISKEY

Irish whiskey is made from malted barley. At the end of the malting process, the germination is halted by drying out the grains in large closed ovens. Since the grains are kept from

coming into contact with the smoke from whatever heat source is used, Irish whiskey won't have the smoky character of a Scotch whisky.

Grains other than barley may be used to make whiskey in Ireland. But this whiskey is generally turned into a neutral grain spirit and used to produce Irish blended whiskies.

SCOTCH WHISKY

The major difference between Irish whiskey and Scotch whisky is that during the Scottish malting process the germinated barley is allowed to be touched by the smoke from the peat fires used to dry the grain out. This produces that unique smoky flavor found, to a certain degree, in all Scotch whisky.

There may be some confusion about the term *single malt* in reference to Scotch whisky. Technically this isn't a term referring to a Scotch made from a single malt, but is, in fact, two terms. Single means that it is a scotch from a single distillery, and malt means that it is only made from malted barley without any neutral grain spirits added. On the other hand, a blended Scotch is a whisky made by blending whiskies from different distilleries. Often this blend includes additional neutral grain spirits. Most, if not all, manufacturers of blended Scotch don't actually have their own distillery. Instead, they rely on a network of smaller local distilleries to provide the whiskies they will use. Some of these manufacturers are starting to make premium blended Scotch that uses malted whiskey without any neutral grain spirits added as filler. These are being marketed as Blended Malt Scotch Whisky.

Rye

AMERICAN WHISKEY

American whiskies are essentially broken down into three main categories: rye, bourbon and blended.

American Rye Whiskey

The first Irish and Scottish immigrants to America continued the distilling practices learned back home. However, they had to make do with whatever they found available here. So, instead of using the traditional barley, they relied on other grains to make their mash. Rye quickly became the grain of choice, and many early American whiskies were made from rye. Rye whiskey dominated the market until Prohibition.

By law, rye whiskey must be made from grains of which is 51% or more are rye.

American Bourbon Whiskey

As the country expanded, settlers once again had to adjust to the grains available for fermentation. Away from the east, corn was the staple and whiskey was made from corn mixed with wheat, rye and other grains.

Kentucky rapidly became a state known for its whiskey. Distilleries in Kentucky and throughout the Midwest made good use of the Mississippi River to distribute their product as far south as New Orleans. There was one problem, however. Corn was harvested

in the fall, and the Mississippi wouldn't be high enough for serious boat traffic until the spring. This meant that whiskey had to sit around in barrels for almost half a year before it could be delivered.

It soon became apparent that this extra time in the barrels produced a new whiskey that was a lot smoother than any before. Bourbon County, Kentucky became associated with this whiskey and people were soon asking specifically for bourbon whiskey.

By law, bourbon whiskey must be made from grains of which is 51% or more are corn.

From Rye to Bourbon

By the time Prohibition ended, many East Coast distillers had already sold their buildings or converted them to other uses. In the Midwest, however, many distillers had simply locked their doors, and were, therefore, quicker to start production again. The result is that today rye whiskey represents a very small portion of the overall whiskey market.

CANADIAN WHISKY

The making of whisky in Canada appears to have started as an afterthought.

Canadian farmers, after harvesting their grain, would rely on a local grist mill to convert that grain into flour used for baking or sold to buy other goods. The grist mill operators naturally charged a fee for their services. Often that fee was a portion of the milled grain.

It wasn't uncommon that the millers found that they had more grain than they could use or sell. Rather than letting this grain sit and spoil, they realized that they could turn it into whisky. Whisky would keep virtually forever, take up less space than grain and meet a certain demand up in the cold northern lands.

Since the millers would have a fairly random collection of different grains, they would make their whisky with more attention to the end result than which specific grains were used. This is why typical Canadian whisky is a blended whisky.

CANADIAN WHISKY AND AMERICAN PROHIBITION

While Prohibition hit American distilleries pretty hard, it was quite a boon to Canadian distillers even though it was illegal to transport and sell their product in America. Canadian whisky, as we all know, found its way into America. Many cocktail books published during, and soon after, Prohibition listed Canadian whisky for use in cocktails that otherwise would have called for American bourbon or rye. To this day, many people refer to Canadian whisky as *rye* because of the confusion that arose during Prohibition.

Gin

Most spirits are defined by the main component of their fermented base. Gin, however, is defined by what is added during the distillation process.

MAKING GIN

As most people know, dried juniper berries are the defining ingredient in gin. The other ingredients are the choice of the distillery.

Things like lemon peel, orange peel, anise, orris root, angelica root, cardamom, coriander, licorice root, cinnamon, almond, lavender and cassia are some of the more common ingredients. Some gins include rose petals, cucumber, mint, dried apples and even hops.

Gin starts out with a neutral spirit, which is almost, but not quite, pure alcohol. Carefully chosen botanicals are then added. The mixture is soaked for a time and then distilled again. The resulting spirit includes many flavor components of the macerated botanicals.

History

Holland's Franciscus Sylvius is usually credited with the invention of gin in the 17th century. Of course this could be debated since juniper berries had long been used as a medicinal treatment, and had already been combined with ales, wines and other alcohols as a way of facilitating their use. But Dr. Sylvius appears to be the first to refer to the drink as *jenever/genever* and so the scales seem to tip in his favor.

The first gins were made in the Netherlands. At first, sugar or other sweeteners were added to the gin to help mask the impurities that resulted from the shoddy distillation of the neighborhood stills.

Because the Dutch government had imposed taxes on imported spirits but not those distilled locally, the cheap price of gin made it almost too popular. The result was rampant drunkenness accompanied by the various social problems that go hand-in-hand with excessive public drinking.

Nicknamed *Dutch Courage*, gin was quickly adopted by the English. By the mid-1800s, thanks to the invention of the column still which could produce a neutral spirit of far higher quality, a new gin style known as *London Dry* developed. London Dry required no sweetener to mask imperfections. The popularity of gin continued to rise, and it didn't take long for it to become a favorite ingredient in cocktails.

BATHTUB GIN

During Prohibition, gin got a bit of a bum rap. Since gin is basically alcohol with added flavorings, gangster entrepreneurs entered into the illegal manufacturing of gin in great numbers. They would often take high-proof grain alcohol, add flavor concentrates to it, water it down and present it as gin. This concoction earned the nickname *bathtub gin*. There are, of course, various problems with this approach. It's about the same as making wine by simply adding grape juice to alcohol.

The Cocktailian Spirit

Arguably, gin is one of the best spirits to make cocktails. Unfortunately, it also appears that most drinkers tend to shy away from it. I think that the reason for this is quite simple. All

of the base spirits have an ongoing tradition of being taken straight. It isn't uncommon to take shots or snifters of brandy, rum, whiskey, tequila or vodka. However, you never hear of someone asking for a snifter or shot of gin. The reason is quite simple: gin really isn't intended to be drunk by itself. It not only needs to be mixed with other flavors, but actually shines when done properly. Most experienced bartenders love to work with gin because it provides an exciting palate of flavors to complement other ingredients.

Tequila

Let's start off by setting the record straight. You will *not* find a worm in a bottle of tequila, unless, of course, you put it there yourself.

As we've already seen, spirits always start out as some product that has been fermented and then distilled. With gin and vodka it doesn't matter what the original product is, but with the rest, it does.

An agave farm, Mexico

Tequila starts out as the fermented sap of the agave plant which is then distilled. That's almost the whole story, but not quite.

Mescal

Frankly, labeling this section *tequila* is like labeling the brandy section *cognac*. Instead we should have named this section *mescal* (mezcal in Spanish), which is the name applied to any spirit made from the fermented sap of the agave plant. In order to be labeled *tequila,* the mescal needs to be made in the Jalisco region of Mexico, and it has to be made from at least 51% blue agave. Premium producers will use 100% blue agave, and will proudly state so on their label.

For many years, mescal had a poor reputation in America because the quality of the imports was extremely poor, far poorer then those staying in Mexico. Some imported mescals tried various marketing gimmicks to drive sales. One gimmick was to add a worm to the bottle thinking that this would help differentiate it from its competitors. Remember, of course, this is not just mescal we're talking about but poor quality mescal, which is about as far removed from tequila as you can get.

Today, quality mescals can still be hard to find without taking a trip to Mexico. However, with a little sleuthing, you can find mescals every bit as good, if not better, than their tequila cousins.

Agave

At the heart of both mescal and tequila is the agave plant. It's a common misconception that it's a cactus. It's not. Like a cactus, agave is classified as a succulent. It looks like an aloe vera plant even though it's not part of that genus either.

When an agave plant is harvested, it's the piña--the heart--at the center of the plant which is brought back to the distillery. This is roasted in large ovens to convert the starches to sugar. The roasted piña is then shredded to release its juices. The juices are fermented

before the distillation process continues much the same way as with other spirits.

Tequila Styles

When buying tequila, you will find several different styles. The three main styles are Blanco (Silver), Reposado (Rested) and Añejo (Aged).

Blanco tequila is unaged tequila. It has a bright vegetal flavor since it hasn't spent any time in barrels to mellow its flavors. Reposado tequila has been aged in oak barrels for at least two months, but not more than a year. This short time in oak will mellow the flavor slightly and add a little golden color to it. Añejo refers to tequila aged in oak barrels for more than a year but less than three. This extended time in oak will greatly mature the flavors, bringing an almost brandy-like flavor to the tequila.

There are some other important designations for tequila. One most commonly seen is *Gold*. This refers to an unaged tequila which has been colored and flavored--usually with caramel--in order to make it look and taste like an aged tequila. Most gold tequilas are also what is referred to as *mixto* tequilas. These aren't made from 100% blue agave and, in most cases, aren't even made from 100% agave. Instead some sugar is added to the agave piña to boost the available sugars for the fermentation process.

I generally prefer to use a silver tequila in cocktails. It provides a very

distinctive tequila flavor which, when combined well with other ingredients, is an excellent way to celebrate this spirit.

While mescal and tequila have been produced in Mexico since the 1500s, they weren't recognized ingredients for cocktails or mixed drinks until Prohibition, a time period when Americans were looking both north and south for replacements for their beloved American whiskey.

Vodka

The history of vodka is both very old and very new. Distillation techniques were traveling around the known world in the 1400s and 1500s resulting in brandy from Europe, rum from the Caribbean Islands, whiskey from Ireland and Scotland and gin from the Netherlands and England. Meanwhile, Slavic communities were producing what was commonly referred to as *woda, voda* or variations thereof, which essentially means *dear little water.*

OLD VERSUS NEW

Modern day vodka is exemplified by its clarity and purity. Highly efficient column stills are used to generate the almost pure alcohol which is the basis for all vodkas. In the early days, distillation was instead achieved with pot stills, which were nowhere as effective as the later column stills. Therefore, the original vodkas bore little similarity to what we think of

INTRODUCTION

as vodka today. In fact, vodka would have been a generic term used to refer to any distilled spirit, regardless of what it was distilled from or what it tasted like. As distillation techniques gradually improved, focus was paid to clarifying the spirit. When column distillation finally came onto the scene, vodka manufacturing was quickly revolutionized.

MAKING VODKA

Unlike brandy, rum, tequila or whiskey, vodka can be made from anything fermentable. Most people think of vodka as being made from potatoes, but most vodka is made from grain, which is far more cost effective. However, vodka is also made from grapes and sugar. It has even been made from milk!

Once a product has been fermented to produce some level of alcohol, it is then distilled through extremely efficient column stills in order to increase the alcohol level to almost, but not quite, 100%. It will usually be filtered to try to remove any additional contaminants left after distillation. The result is an extremely pure product.

To this point, the process is very similar to making gin. For gin, you macerate the alcohol in juniper and other botanicals. After distillation, water is added to bring the liquid to bottle strength around 40% ABV. For vodka, you skip the maceration and distillation and go straight to adding water to bring things down to bottle strength.

VODKA'S LITTLE SECRET

As we've seen, whiskey is distilled from grain, any grain. If most vodka is also distilled from grain, why isn't it a whiskey? The answer lies in the distillation. To have the distinctive characteristics necessary to be called bourbon whiskey, you can't distill higher than 75% alcohol. If you go higher than that, you have to call it simply whiskey. However, if you distill higher than 95% alcohol, you become vodka.

The bottled strength of vodka needs to be brought down to about 40% alcohol. This is done by adding water. Since you are starting with something that is almost, but not quite, pure alcohol, you need to add almost 60% water to turn it into vodka. Perhaps the most important decision a distiller will make is selecting the water, which can have a dramatic effect on the overall flavor of the product.

VODKA IN AMERICA

Prior to Prohibition, vodka was practically non-existent as a cocktail ingredient. Even after Prohibition, vodka failed to make an impact. The American introduction of Smirnoff's near the end of the 1930s might have been a turning point, but before it had a chance for success, World War II intervened.

Following the war, Smirnoff again focused on capturing the American market. Vodka sales increased gradually into the 1950s when it was promoted as a replacement for the gin in martinis as well as other spirits that might be used in cocktails. The idea caught on and vodka sales began to take off. By 1976 vodka was outselling all other spirits.

Distilleries manufacturing vodka have great advantages over those making other spirits. Unlike most spirits, vodka can be created anywhere, out of anything and, most importantly, can be bottled immediately after distillation without the added time and expense of barrel aging.

TRAINING WHEELS

Used in cocktails, vodka can be seen as the liquid equivalent of training wheels. To those just discovering the joys of cocktails and mixed drinks, the unfamiliar and complex flavors of spirits like gin, whiskey and tequila can sometimes be a little too jarring. On the other hand, vodka has the bite of alcohol without the complexity of other flavors that might puzzle new drinkers. Further, you can easily add vodka to almost any otherwise non-alcoholic drink, and it suddenly becomes an *adult* beverage.

INFUSIONS

Lately, vodka has been used to create various flavor infusions. Alcohol has the wonderful capability of being a great medium for extracting flavors from various products. By simply adding a fruit, spice, herb or even vegetable to vodka, you will have, in a few short days, a product which has taken on some of the component's flavor characteristics. You can then use this mixture to make many interesting and unique mixed drinks.

Other Cocktail Ingredients

The Bartender's Pantry

Spirits are only the starting point for making a cocktail or mixed drink. It's what you add to that spirit which turns it into a cocktail and defines its culinary identity.

Originally, the palate of ingredients added to various drinks was relatively limited. Some ingredients just didn't exist, but many hadn't been embraced yet by the bartenders of the day.

Initially, simple sweeteners and citrus juices were the stock of the day, along with a variety of fruits and berries used as garnishes, sometimes with abandon.

Some recipes, most notably for a punch, called for the addition of spices. You might say they were added to *spice up* the drink. Perhaps this led someone to think of adding bitters to a drink, particularly since some bartenders considered bitters to be liquid spice concentrates.

Over time, additional ingredients made their ways into various drinks, and with each new addition, the culinary potentials of the drinks would take radical leaps forward. It's

Liqueurs

as if a cook who had been limited to onions, potatoes and chicken suddenly discovered the wonders of salt, cumin and butter. That's when the genie finally gets released from the bottle.

Today, there are hundreds of different spirituous liqueurs, wines, bitters, juices and various other ingredients lending their character to a wide assortment of drinks. Understanding the roles each ingredient can play in a drink is one of the cornerstones of the bartender's craft.

Let's take a look at some, but not nearly all, of the various ingredients used to prepare the cocktail recipes included here. It's worth taking some time to understand these ingredients so you'll be better prepared to make these cocktails. Also, understanding the ingredients will allow you to substitute one ingredient for another when the situation calls for it.

Cordials and Syrups

Sweeteners have long played a big roll in mixed drinks. Initially used as a way to mask unwanted flavors, they gradually and rightfully were seen as a major element in the all important balancing act that can make these drinks magical.

The essence of whatever drink you are having or making is the balance of flavors. Drinks which are overly sweet or sour are mere pretenders, hoping that screaming their flavors loudly will prevent people from recognizing that

there isn't any craftsmanship behind them.

The first sweeteners--most likely, fruits and berries--added their natural sweetness, flavors and tartness to various drinks. When sugar became more readily available, it quickly supplanted other sweeteners as the sweetener of choice. This was an easy decision because sugar stored for a long time and it added only sweetness to the equation, thus allowing its effect on the drink to be controlled better.

Also, the availability of sugar led to an increased production of cordials and flavored syrups whose gains in popularity were aided by their cheaper prices.

In the mid-1800s, sweeteners in addition to sugar included orgeat syrup (a sweet syrup made from barley and later almonds prepared with an extract of orange flowers and sugar), maraschino liqueur (made using the marascas cherry), curaçao a.k.a curaçoa (made using the peel of sour oranges) and various berry syrups play the role of sweetener. Over time, the landscape expanded until today, there are hundreds of possible choices for sweetening a drink.

Cordials, Liqueurs and Crèmes

You will often see the terms cordial and liqueur used interchangeably. Each refers to a sweet and usually alcoholic beverage with a fruit, herb or sometimes spice flavor. To provide some level of separation, some countries put specific requirements on each.

Amaretto

Getting its name not from almond, or even *amore* (Italian for "love"), the root of the name amaretto is *amaro*, which means bitter in Italian. Thus amaretto means *a little bitter*. The flavor comes from almond and/or peach pits soaked in alcohol and then sweetened.

Coffee Liqueur

There are a wide variety of coffee liqueurs on the market, but Kahlúa is the most widely known. Basically, Kahlúa is made from coffee, vanilla and various secret spices in a neutral grain base. Another well-known coffee liqueur Tia Maria is owned today by Pernod-Ricard, the same company that owns Kahlúa.

Cointreau

(See curaçao)

Crème de Cacao

There's little doubt that chocolate is just about everyone's favorite flavor, and crème de cacao is aimed straight at chocolate lovers. Its flavor comes primarily from the cocoa bean, usually with some vanilla added. You'll see it coming in both clear and dark brown. Unlike the artificially colored curaçao, there are slight differences in the manufacturing of clear, which has a slightly lighter flavor, and dark crème de cacao. The difference isn't terribly noticeable, however, so the clear is usually recommended when you make cocktails. Using the dark will turn every cocktail a muddy brown.

Crème de Cassis

A specialty of the Burgundy region of France, Crème de Cassis is made from blackcurrants (*cassis* in French) which have been crushed and soaked in alcohol before straining and sweetening with sugar. Crème de Cassis is most notably used in the drinks Kir and Kir Royale.

Curaçao and Other Orange Cordials

It's likely that the most popular sweet cordial flavor in cocktails is orange. It goes by many names and comes in several forms. One of the first was curaçao, today often called orange curaçao. It's a relatively simple orange flavored liqueur. Originally curaçao used brandy as its base spirit, but now it generally uses a neutral grain spirit. Triple sec evolved in the early 1800s as a cleaner, more refined version of orange curaçao.

Most brands of both curaçao and triple sec are relatively inexpensive, and their quality is usually reflected in their price. If you're looking for premium brands, you'll want to pick up Grand Marnier (which has a brandy base) to use as your orange curaçao and Cointreau (which has a neutral grain spirit base) to use for recipes calling for triple sec.

When looking for curaçao, you will often find it in clear, orange and blue varieties. Given that there's no difference in flavor, I always recommend either the clear or orange variety since the blue will only work in cocktails intentionally meant to be blue (in other words, very few).

Grand Marnier

(See curaçao)

Limoncello

As orange lovers have orange curaçao and its variations, lemon lovers have limoncello. This is a traditional Italian liqueur, often made at home. It's made by macerating (a fancy word for soaking) thinly sliced lemons or just the lemon peels in grain alcohol (vodka) for several weeks, straining and then adding a simple sweetening syrup.

Maraschino Liqueur

Once commonly used in a variety of cocktails, Maraschino liqueur gradually disappeared as the cocktails which used it fell into obscurity. With the classic cocktail resurgence, Maraschino liqueur is seeing a radical and well deserved comeback. Like curaçao, it is essentially a sweet fruit liqueur flavored, as the name implies, from cherries. Its character is less sweet but more complex than curaçao since the flavor comes not just from the

fruit but the seeds as well. This results in a slightly diverse set of flavors that seem to provide hints of chocolate, vanilla and almonds.

Maraschino liqueur should not be confused with modern maraschino cherries. There is no similarity between the two, and heaven help the bartender who substitutes the juice from a jar of maraschino cherries for maraschino liqueur in a cocktail.

Sloe Gin

Today, most available versions of Sloe Gin are pale imitations of what they once were. True sloe gin is made by soaking sloe berries a.k.a. blackthorn in gin that has been sweetened with sugar and often flavored with cinnamon, cloves and almond. This is left to soak for weeks, if not months, before straining and bottling. Traditionally this was something which would be made at home.

Triple Sec

(See curaçao)

Syrups

For the most part, syrups play the same role in a drink as cordials. Both provide sweetening and a useful flavor component. The main difference is, of course, syrup is non-alcoholic.

These days, it's easy to find a broad range of flavored syrups in grocery stores. They've become popular with the growth of coffee shops and the flavored coffee drinks that are often their signature drink. While not all syrups will be as good in a cocktail as they might be in your coffee, they still provide a wealth of potential for experimenting.

Elderflower Syrup

Once a rather popular ingredient for cocktails in London bars, this product hasn't really crossed the Atlantic. Made from the flowers of the elder (a.k.a elderberry) tree with some lemon juice and sweetening, it has a floral flavor with citrus notes. Recently an elderflower flavored liqueur called St. Germain has entered the market. This will be a lot easier to find in the US and Canada than elderflower syrup.

Falernum

It's difficult to categorize falernum. Is it a cordial or a syrup? Some versions are alcoholic and others are not. When it's alcoholic, the alcohol content is usually quite low. To complicate matters more, falernum is generally hard to find. It's basically an almond flavored syrup with the addition of clove, ginger, lime and a few other spices.

Grenadine

True grenadine is made from pomegranate juice. Unfortunately modern grenadine is usually just a simple syrup with added red food coloring and a little citric acid. It's definitely worth your effort to search

out a real grenadine. Or, you can make your own grenadine by simmering pomegranate juice until it has reached half its original volume and then add an equal amount of sugar to match the volume of juice.

Orgeat

The proliferation of coffee shop syrups hasn't made it easy to find orgeat, which is an important ingredient in the Mai Tai, one of the most popular cocktails from the Tiki era. You can, however, easily replace orgeat with almond syrup, which is much easier to find. The difference between the two is that orgeat is typically cloudy while almond syrup is clear and orgeat includes a small amount of orange flower water.

Simple Syrup

A first encounter with simple syrup as an ingredient in a cocktail recipe usually causes a certain level of confusion. To complicate matters, it's an unlikely product to be found at a liquor or grocery store.

Simple syrup is exactly what the name says, *simple*. It's easy to make by dissolving sugar in water. The specific ratios vary from person to person. Some prefer using equal amounts by volume of water and sugar, while others use twice as much sugar as water. The 2-to-1 version is often referred to as *rich* simple syrup.

Sugar is dissolved in water in one of

Aromatized wines

two ways. The most traditional method is to bring the water to a simmer and then stir in the sugar until it dissolves. Allow it to cool, and bottle it. You can also combine the sugar and water in a bottle, close it tight, shake it until it's completely dissolved and then shake it a little more for good measure.

Either way, if the syrup is stored at room temperature for more than a day, add about an ounce of vodka per quart to prevent mold from accumulating.

Aromatized Wines

Wines have a much older history than spirits. Many of the oldest wines probably had more in common with vermouth than with modern wines.

When fermentation wasn't as well understood as it is today, it was unlikely that the quality would be good enough to allow wine to be enjoyed as-is. The Greeks and Romans are known to have added fruits,

86

herbs and even salt-water to their wines as a flavoring agent. Since wine was believed to be medicinal, it was common for the additives to support or enhance the desired benefits.

Aromatized wines are the result of adding various herbs and botanicals to a wine. It's also common to add some brandy or other spirit, which allows them to be called *fortified* wines. These additions result in a wine that is less fragile then normal, one that will travel better since it isn't as susceptible to going bad soon after opening. The added alcohol will forestall the onset of oxidation for a while and the botanicals will help mask the taste of wine going bad.

This is not to say that an aromatized wine is shelf stable. When possible you should store an open bottle in the refrigerator or plan to use it within a week. After that time, not only will the flavor start to deteriorate, but wine left out too long will begin tossing sediments that are visible as black or white specks in your drink.

Dubonnet

Originally formulated in Chamberly, France, by Joseph Dubonnet in 1846, Dubonnet wasn't introduced to Americans until after Prohibition. Usually Dubonnet is sipped on the rocks with a twist of lemon, but there are a few cocktails such as the Opera, Deshler and Zaza that call for its use.

Today, the Dubonnet available in America is made in Kentucky and is slightly different from the version made by the Dubonnet company in France. Dubonnet comes in both a red (*rouge*) and a white (*blanc*) version, with the red being the most common version for use in cocktails.

Lillet

Created in the late 1800s in Podensac, France, this aromatized wine includes an assortment of fruits, herbs and spices in its proprietary recipe. One of the spices is quinine, the same ingredient found in tonic water, and this gives an ever-so-slight bitterness to its taste. Around 1980, the formula for Lillet was changed to lower the quinine content for a more approachable flavor.

Lillet comes in both a white (*blanc*) and red (*rouge*) version. The wine used is either a white or red Bordeaux, and both versions use the same flavorings. On the other hand, vermouth uses white wine for both its red and white versions. In this case, the difference is provided by varying the herbs.

Vermouth

Vermouth is the most frequent aromatized wine in cocktail recipes. The name comes from the German *wermut* which means wormwood. Wormwood has long been considered a plant possessing great medicinal properties. This is, perhaps, because of its very bitter taste which would seem to have no other value. It was a fairly common flavoring component in many herbal wines. Usually vermouth would be made in small batches for either personal or local use. The first commercially made vermouth appears to be from Italy. Like most of the vermouth style wines then, it was sweet and red even though the wine it was made from was, in fact, white. The red color came from the flavorings used.

The French weren't too far behind the Italians. Joseph Noilly's version helped define French vermouth as being white and dry.

Although Italian and French vermouth date to the early half of the 1800s, vermouth didn't find its way into American cocktail recipes until the later half of the century. The Italian sweet red vermouth became so popular that whenever recipes called for vermouth, it was assumed that meant Italian vermouth. If the intended ingredient was French vermouth, the recipe would specifically say so.

Today, the notion of *Italian* and *French* as designations of different vermouths has been eliminated since nearly all producers of vermouth make both the sweet/red style as well as the dry/white style. So, *sweet* and *dry* are the typical ways to designate vermouth today.

Bitters

Bitters used in a cocktail can come in two different varieties. Cocktail bitters, meant to be used sparingly, usually comes in a very small bottle with a dasher top. Digestive bitters, which are used in amounts you can actually measure, may be drunk straight. The line between the two can get a little hazy.

Cocktail Bitters

Because we've mentioned cocktail bitters so frequently, you've probably realized how important we feel they are to the cocktail. Unfortunately, they are often slighted by the majority of bartenders. Once there were dozens of different cocktail bitters available to the classically trained bartender. Today, depending on how you count them, you'll find just over a dozen varieties. Still, the situation is a lot better than it was just a few years ago.

Bitters are essentially a combination of multiple herbs and spices, which are soaked in alcohol to extract very concentrated flavors before bottling. They are usually alcoholic and are not normally intended to be taken straight. Their flavor is very intense, but, when used in small dashes, they aromatize a cocktail and support and enhance its flavors.

Most cocktail bitters are made from a proprietary recipe, meaning that, even though the recipe uses dozens of different complex ingredients, only three or so living people know the recipe. Over the years, there have been a few less distinctive bitters made by several different companies much the same way that tomato ketchup is

INTRODUCTION

today. One of the more popular generic brands was orange bitters.

Angostura Bitters

For the longest time, this appeared to be the only bitters generally known. Its distinctive oversized label provided easy recognition.

Due to the enhanced interest in classic cocktails, Angostura has recently released their version of orange bitters, the only other bitters they have ever made.

Fee Brother's Bitters

The Fee Brother's Company of Rochester, New York, has been producing syrups, cordials and

bitters for making cocktails since 1863. During Prohibition they produced a variety of non-alcoholic products intended to make non-alcoholic versions of favorite cocktails.

They currently make several different bitters: Aromatic, Barrel Aged Aromatic, Orange, Peach, Lemon, Grapefruit and Mint.

Peychaud's Bitters

Antoine Peychaud started selling his proprietary bitters in New Orleans around 1830, and, while there were various bits of drama which sometimes surrounded their production, they have been generally available since then. Their popularity is perhaps limited to the fact that only a few

Bitters

cocktails specifically call for them, the most famous being the Sazerac.

Regan's Orange Bitters #6

Noted author and cocktail historian Gary Regan was so disappointed about his inability to find orange bitters anywhere that he took it on himself to come up with his own recipe. After four variations he found a recipe he liked and decided to make a commercial version. It took two more variations before the federal government approved it.

The Bitter Truth

The Bitter Truth, a small company in Germany, is making several different bitters that are well-received by bartenders in Europe as well as those few American bartenders who can get them. Regrettably difficult to find in the U.S., the bitters include an Aromatic, Orange and Lemon. The company is also trying to perfect the recipe for Boker's bitters, the brand of bitters called for by Jerry Thomas in his 1862 recipe book.

Digestive Bitters

Digestive Bitters can often be difficult to classify since some may be thought of as apéritifs. However, an *apéritif* should stimulate the appetite and be had before a meal while a *digestif* is had following the meal to help settle things down.

I usually consider *apéritifs*, which include aromatized wines, to be lighter

of the two in flavor. On the other hand, a *digestif* is a complex, almost overpowering, flavor that will put your taste buds down for the count. There are a lot of different products in this category, far more than we really need to concern ourselves with now. Here's a quick description of the most popular and/or most important ones.

Absinthe

Also known as the *green fairy*, absinthe was banned almost world wide back in the early 1900s. Feared for its supposed hallucinogenic properties, we now know that the supposed effects were simply part of a successful smear campaign led by the temperance union of the day. Serious misunderstanding about absinthe has ruled since then.

The flavor of absinthe is similar to black licorice, coming not actually from licorice, but, rather, from anise and fennel. After absinthe was banned, pastis was developed as a replacement.

In Europe, the drinking of absinthe was almost ritualistic. First, water was slowly dripped onto a sugar cube. The sweetened water than dripped into a glass containing absinthe waiting below. The clear cold water, when slowly combined with the green absinthe, would turn opalescent, capable like an opal of displaying different colors from within its milky depths. This was referred to as a *louche* from the Old French for squinting. This process was known as the absinthe drip and is unique to absinthe. Perhaps this is part of its charm.

In the 1990s poor quality absinthe, which wouldn't *louche* or display different colors, was being sold in Europe. In an attempt to find their own absinthe ritual, some contemporary bartenders introduced the notion of a flaming sugar cube. While providing a bit of a show, it does nothing at all to improve bad absinthe and will actually ruin good absinthe. So, it's not an advisable method to use.

In the U.S., the absinthe drip never really caught on. Instead, absinthe was used much the same way as cocktail bitters were: just a dash or two to add a little extra flavor component to the drink.

Absinthe has been gradually making a comeback, and recently several brands were approved for distribution as well as manufacture in the U.S.

Amer Picon

Looking through older cocktail manuals, you will often encounter Amer Picon as an ingredient. Unfortunately this product has pretty much disappeared from the American market and is even difficult to find in Europe where it is made.

The Torani Company, the same folks who make coffee syrups, make Torani Amer, their version of Amer Picon. It's currently the only choice we have in the U.S. The flavor is robust and multi-layered with a definite orange

character. Some feel that it is even a reasonable substitute for orange bitters.

The few recipes calling for Amer Picon in the recipe section are included in the hope that Amer Picon will again become available.

Bénédictine

As the name might imply, Bénédictine has monastic roots. The original recipe was devised in 1510 by Dom Bernardo Vincelli, who combined twenty-seven different plants and spices to create

his special elixir. It was presumed to be a health tonic and was produced by the Bénédictine monks for that purpose. During the turmoil of the French Revolution, production ceased and the monks never took it up again. The recipe was eventually sold, and then subsequently lost. Then in 1863, Alexandre Le Grand rediscovered the recipe, and, after considerable work, started producing it again.

The recipe for Bénédictine is a closely guarded secret, but a few of its ingredients are known. These include ambrette, cinnamon, cardamom, saffron, vanilla, nutmeg, hyssop, myrrh, coriander, lemon balm, thyme, clove and tea. Its complex flavor is both bitter and sweet with various complex spicy undertones.

You're probably more likely to come across a bottle of B&B in bars today than Bénédictine itself. B&B, which is a mixture of half Bénédictine and half brandy, has become one of the most popular ways to drink Bénédictine. However, given a choice, I prefer to see a bottle of Bénédictine instead of, or in addition to, B&B. With a bottle of Bénédictine you can easily make a B&B as well as any other cocktail that uses Bénédictine, but with B&B you can just make—well—B&B.

Campari

Often referred to as the most bitter of bitters, the flavor of Campari can be unpalatable at first, but with gradual introduction it soon takes on amazing and tantalizing complexities.

Campari originated in Italy in the 1860s. Gaspare Campari devised a recipe consisting of 60 different ingredients, which, as you might expect, remains a closely guarded secret.

Perhaps the most popular Campari cocktail is the Negroni, with the Americano close behind.

Chartreuse

Like Bénédictine, Chartreuse was developed in a monastery, but, unlike Bénédictine, it is still being produced there.

The original recipe started as an *Elixir of Life* recipe given to the Charthusian monks at Vauvert in 1605. The recipe was sent to the monastery's herbalist to decipher the complex formula. He died before he could finish, and the task was handed to his apprentice to complete. It took until 1737 to derive a workable recipe and start producing Chartreuse.

Today Chartreuse comes in a number of colors with green Chartreuse being the most common in cocktails.

Cynar

In some ways, the flavor of Cynar is similar to that of Campari. However, it is slightly more subdued. Cynar has a dark brown color while Campari is a bright transparent red. We also know an important ingredient of Cynar, because it proudly sports it on its label: the noble artichoke! At first that flavor might seem elusive, but in time you can see that flavor intermixed with all the other herbs and spices which give it its complex and robust flavor.

Fernet Branca

Like Campari, Fernet Branca has the sort of flavor only a mother could love. It was originally formulated by Maria Scala in 1845 as a medicine. Scala then married into the Branca family and its manufacture is still controlled by the Branca family.

While all of its ingredients are not known, it is known to include aloe, cardamom, chamomile, cinchona bark, columbus, galangal, gentian, myrrh, rhubarb, saffron and zedoary. Like many Italian bitters, it is intended to be taken after a meal as a *digestif*. However, when encountered by a younger crowd, it often turns into a manly *right of passage* type drink downed quickly as a shot. Today, Fernet Branca is extremely popular in San Francisco, where they drink more of it than anywhere else in the world.

Pastis

When absinthe was banned in France in 1915, a substitute was needed. The two most popular manufacturers in France at the time were Pernod and Ricard. They both eventually came to market with what they felt was a suitable replacement, even though

their products were pre-sweetened and lacked some of the complexities of real absinthe. It was Ricard who first coined the term *pastis* to refer to this type of product. Even though the two companies eventually merged into Pernod-Ricard, Pernod and Ricard are still marketed as separate, but extremely similar, products.

Juices

Juices of one sort or another have been a constant component of the mixed drink. Technically and historically, juices don't belong in a cocktail. But, by the later half of the 1800s, that orthodoxy was thrown out the window. With the potential of an ever-expanding list of available ingredients growing, it was difficult to place too many restrictions on the creativity of the bartenders of the day.

Whenever possible, fresh juices should be seen as the only option for making a quality cocktail. Even if the preparation requires a little extra work and expense, the difference is measurable.

If you don't have time to fresh squeeze your juices for each drink, you can prepare some juice ahead of time. Remember, though, that juices will start going bitter in a short amount of time. You should measure a juice's lifetime in hours not days, and always keep juices well chilled.

Many juices have a fairly aggressive flavor that can quickly overpower a drink if too much is used. For this reason I always highly recommend measuring cocktails carefully. Keep in mind that a recipe calling for something along the lines of "the juice of half a lemon" is imprecise and should always be avoided. The amount of juice from one fruit to the next can vary enough to throw the drink off.

Cranberry Juice

I'm not sure I'd ever recommend fresh squeezed cranberry juice. Even if it were possible I doubt it would have the results needed. Typical recipes calling for cranberry juice have been developed with commercial juice in mind. Commercial cranberry juices aren't pure. They are, rather, a combination of cranberry and other fruit juices to make what is known as a cranberry juice cocktail. Squeezing your own juice would provide a far different result in a mixed drink.

Grapefruit Juice

Grapefruits are usually larger than most hand juicers can accommodate. If this is a problem for you, try cutting the fruit into quarters and juice each quarter individually.

Lemon and Lime

These are perhaps the most common juices used in cocktails. They provide an excellent balance to sweetening ingredients.

You should keep plenty of fresh lemons and limes on hand, not only for juicing but for garnishing as well. A lemon twist is the most common cocktail garnish. Remember that fruit more than a few days old will have a loose skin which is harder to cut with a channel knife.

Orange Juice

Unlike lemon and lime juice, orange juice is seen as a high demand consumer product, and one which is drunk by itself. This means that some

of the commercially available bottled orange juices are pretty good and provide a familiar flavor. Still, fresh orange juice has a noticeably brighter and livelier flavor.

Because orange juice has a tendency to flatten and mellow flavors in a cocktail, you should be very judicious in its use. If you encounter a recipe using orange juice and you don't like it, try reducing the orange juice and see how that affects the taste.

Pineapple Juice

Squeezing your own pineapple juice can be a real chore unless you have the right equipment. Fresh juice is still better, but because it is so hard to squeeze properly, bottled or canned pineapple juice is acceptable.

Like orange juice, pineapple juice has a tendency to easily dominate a cocktail.

Tomato Juice

Like pineapples, tomatoes are difficult to squeeze for fresh juice. Most recipes are designed to use commercially available products.

Sour Mix

Finally, I need to say that at no time should you ever consider using sour mix in your cocktails.

Some drinks like the whiskey sour are made with an equal measure of simple syrup and lemon juice. Sour mix was created as a pre-made short cut for mixing those drinks. The idea was to save time by having the mix already at hand. Then, when someone ordered a Whiskey Sour, you had only two bottles to pour from instead of three. Lazy bartenders would then use the same premix to make Daiquiris (which should use lime juice instead of lemon) and then for a Margarita (which should use lime juice instead of lemon and an orange liqueur instead of a plain simple syrup).

Sour Mix suddenly became the *hammer*, and any drink that needed a sweetening agent and a souring agent of any sort was suddenly seen as the *nail*. Add commercialization to the mix, and instead of a mix of simple syrup and lemon juice, sour mix is being made from high fructose corn syrup, citric acid and a variety of additional flavorings, stabilizers and preservatives.

The Classic Cocktails

The Foundation

Before rattling off a couple hundred cocktail recipes, let's take a look at a few of the basics. These will provide the foundation upon which most of the other drinks you're likely to make are based. By looking at these in detail, you'll be better prepared to tackle recipes that come with few specifics on preparation.

All of these foundation recipes are for drinks that are relatively common. In some cases the presentation differs from what might be served by bartenders today. In these cases I'll explain the differences and why they exist.

We've already discussed the advantages of focusing on one recipe a week. Select your recipe and pick up the necessary ingredients. I'd recommend spending at least a week on each of the drinks in this section and really mastering it. As you master each of these recipes, I'd like to suggest you do a little research. Check alternate recipes online or in other books. Try some of the variations to determine your preferences and always ask yourself, "Why is this better than that?"

Nothing is written in stone. This means that the recipes listed here shouldn't be seen as *the* recipe for any particular drink any more then the recipe for tomato soup you might find in a cookbook should be thought of as the only way tomato soup should be made. It's my intent, however, for you to enjoy every recipe and learn from them how to make the best cocktails possible.

Sidecar

- 2 ounces (60ml) brandy (cognac)
- 1 ounce (30ml) Cointreau
- ½ ounce (15ml) lemon juice

Shake with ice.

Strain into cocktail glass.

Someone new to cocktails may find that many have a flavor profile that's too jarring. The martini is one of the quintessential cocktails, but neophytes may think you're asking them to drink a shot of Tabasco.

This version of the sidecar is a good place to begin to show what real cocktails are all about. I use the word *version* since this isn't the original recipe, nor is likely to be what you'd be served in most bars today.

When it first appeared in print, the sidecar was equal parts cognac, Cointreau and lemon juice. Frankly, I find that this makes a drink that's far too sour for the palate. The first few sips might be fine, but, by the time you get to the end, you're ready to move on to something else.

Beware of the modern Sidecar. It's often just brandy and sour mix, a sad drink by any measure.

The Sidecar was one of the first cocktails that I taught myself. I went through a variety of recipes before settling on this one. I feel that the ratios presented here, specifically using Cointreau and fresh lemon juice, result in a drink that is smooth as velvet and, when you reach the end, you wish you had made just a little more.

Often this drink is served with a sugared rim, but I find that sugared rims are usually a bad idea. Sugared rims give you a sticky finger problem, but more than that, history is on my side. The original Sidecar recipe didn't call for it either.

For research purposes, you may want to pick up a bottle of triple sec, as well as some bottled lemon juice. Try using triple sec instead of Cointreau and the bottled lemon juice instead of fresh. I think you'll taste the difference.

Also, if you find an online recipe using sour mix, try that as well. I'm confident that this will be a lesson quickly learned.

Daiquiri

- 2 ounces (60ml) light rum
- ¾ ounce (22ml) simple syrup
- ½ ounce (15ml) lime juice

Shake with ice and strain into a cocktail glass.

Garnish with a lime slice.

You'll notice that both the Sidecar and the Daiquiri are made with a base spirit, a sweet ingredient and a sour ingredient. This type of drink in a variety of forms is typically called a sour.

The origin of the Daiquiri is an oft-told story. Around 1896, a man named Jennings Cox mixed a drink combining rum, lime juice, sugar and ice. He served it to friends visiting him in Cuba. The drink was named for a nearby town.

There's nothing remarkable to be found in each individual ingredient. They were all extremely common in Cuba and known for hundreds of years. It's a little more remarkable to think that Mr. Cox suddenly decided to combine them. The story, then, may be apocryphal. It's more likely that this drink was a common refreshment in the area, and Mr. Cox simply introduced his visitors to it.

Most people might think of a Daiquiri as a frozen drink, something that has more in common with a frosty Slushee™ than a refined cocktail. Along Bourbon Street in New Orleans, it's common to see banks of frozen drink machines churning out "Daiquiris" of every flavor imaginable.

The frozen daiquiri is something that should be avoided at all costs. A proper alcoholic drink should never remind you of your childhood. That's just wrong.

Margarita

- 1½ ounce (45ml) tequila
- 1 ounce (30ml) Cointreau
- ½ ounce (15ml) lime juice

Shake with ice.

Strain into an ice-filled Old Fashioned glass or a salt-rimmed margarita glass.

For decades, the Margarita has been the most popular cocktail in the world. Is it because it's so closely associated with Mexican cuisine that it might seem disrespectful not to order a Margarita with your meal? Or is it simply that when properly made, it's an excellent drink?

One of the most common origin stories surrounding the Margarita involves Margarita Sames. It seems that while hosting a party in 1948, Ms. Sames created this special drink to serve to her guests. A nice story and it sounds plausible but, unfortunately, there are enough other stories about the origins of the Margarita that you have to take all of them with a grain of salt.

The Margarita, of course, is also in the sour family. Like the Sidecar and Daiquiri, it combines a spirit with both sweet and sour ingredients to produce a well-balanced drink. Looking back at these recipes, you'll note that each uses slightly different ingredients. It's the ingredients and the flavors they reflect that define each carefully prepared drink.

Just as the making of a frozen drink is often the ruin of the Daiquiri, the Margarita is ruined by the use of a commercial sour mix. Of course, it's hard to ignore the fact that, like the Daiquiri, the Margarita is often also considered to be a frozen drink.

Like the Sidecar, the Margarita is commonly served rimmed, but with salt instead of sugar. Fortunately salt won't give you the same sticky finger effect that an improperly sugared rim will. It will, however, put salt in your drink and a rarely pleasant briny mixture at the bottom of your drink.

When you salt the rim of your Margarita, focus on salting just the outside of the glass without getting salt on the inside. This is easily accomplished by rubbing the rim with a lime wedge and then using a spoon to cascade kosher or pickling salt over the outside of the glass with a spoon.

Cosmopolitan

- 1½ ounce (45ml) citrus vodka
- ½ ounce (15ml) Cointreau
- 1 ounce (30ml) cranberry juice
- ¾ ounce (22ml) lime juice

Shake with ice.

Strain into a cocktail glass.

Garnish with lime wedge.

Possibly the Cosmopolitan is suffering from the popularity it achieved in the 1990s. It's still an extremely common drink to order, but for many it's become rather passé.

This is a shame because, properly made, the Cosmopolitan is not only an excellent cocktail but a worthy member of the same family tree as the Sidecar, Margarita and Daiquiri. Like its cousins, the Cosmopolitan uses a base spirit combined with both sour and sweet ingredients to form a carefully balanced result.

Cosmopolitans start running into problems when shortcuts or cost saving measures are put into play. Cointreau is always preferred to triple sec and fresh squeezed lime juice is critical. The thought of using any form of bottled lime juice or sour mix should never be entertained.

The origins of the cosmopolitan have been elusive until recently. Noted author and historian Gary Regan believes he recently uncovered the

scoop when he was put in touch with a woman named Cheryl Cook. It appears that in 1985 Ms. Cook was the first to mix this drink when she worked at the Strand in South Beach, Miami. She was inspired by the recently introduced Absolut Citron and wanted to create a drink utilizing it. She combined this new vodka with triple sec, Rose's lime juice and just enough cranberry juice to make it "oh so pretty in pink."

The original version of the cocktail evolved into its modern form through the efforts of Dale DeGroff and Toby Cecchini. Both focused on elevating the quality of the drink by using Cointreau instead of triple sec and replacing Rose's lime juice with fresh lime juice. If you want to compare the two versions, please do. I'll think you'll quickly see why the version presented here is the one that quality bars use.

Old Fashioned

- •1 sugar cube (1 teaspoon/5ml)
- •1 teaspoon (5ml) water
- •2 dashes Angostura bitters
- •2 ounces (60ml) American rye or bourbon whiskey

Muddle sugar, water and bitters together until the sugar is mostly dissolved.

Fill glass with ice and then add the whiskey.

Garnish with a twist of orange peel, and a cherry.

Serve with straws.

According to many stories, the Old Fashioned was invented at the Pendennis Club in Louisville, Kentucky. Unfortunately, history doesn't bare this out. Cocktail researcher David Wondrich uncovered a reference to a drink named the *Old Fashioned* in an 1880 edition of the Chicago Tribune. The Pendennis Club wouldn't open until the next year.

In truth, the Old Fashioned is a "whiskey cocktail made the old fashioned way." By the late 1800s, cocktails had changed so much that somebody from 1810 would no longer recognize one. So, in many ways, the Old Fashioned represents the *original* cocktail.

Unfortunately, this drink is so rarely ordered that most bartenders no longer know how to make it properly. The result tends to be pretty bad.

If you're at all familiar with the Old Fashioned, you may have expected the recipe to mention muddling a slice of orange and cherry with the drink at the start. However, this is a fairly new addition to the drink, and it quite likely marks the beginning of the downfall. The muddled orange may provide an orange flavor that works well with the whiskey, but it also adds bits of citrus pulp to the drink which will clog the straws. Properly adding an orange twist at the end--remember to cut it over the drink--will add a hint of that citrus flavor without the pulp. The muddled cherry only results in a mangled carcass. I'd rather leave the cherry unmolested as a garnish. You might also see bartenders topping off the drink with water or club soda. This is overkill since the water in the recipe makes a simple syrup and should be just enough to do the job. If you'd like, you could use simple syrup and omit the sugar and water all together.

Martini (Sweet)

Martini (Dry)

The Classic Martini

- 2½ ounces (75ml) gin
- ¾ ounce (22ml) sweet or dry vermouth
- Dash orange bitters

Stir with ice.

Strain into a cocktail glass.

Garnish with a lemon twist.

Historians continue to debate the origins of the Martini, both who first made it as well as where the name itself comes from. Perhaps less attention should be paid to history and more to making the drink properly.

This recipe may seem strange at first, since it not only includes a lot more vermouth than you've come to expect but it also includes orange bitters. In addition, it doesn't specify which type of vermouth to use. So, I'd like to recommend that you try this first with sweet vermouth instead of the dry you might be used to, since this is the way the drink was originally made.

Any bartender or consumer prior to Prohibition would readily recognize and accept this recipe. Back then many cocktails were made with sweet vermouth, and, if you wanted a variation using dry vermouth instead, you would ask for a *dry* cocktail. Making the recipe above with sweet vermouth would be a true Martini, while making it with dry vermouth would make it a dry Martini.

Like all cocktails, a Martini should represent an artful balance of ingredients. No one ingredient should overshadow another. The modern Martini, however, is often made with merely the vapors of vermouth, and this clearly wouldn't be enough to stand up to the flavor of a good gin. If a Martini is properly made, you shouldn't be able to tell where the gin stops and the vermouth begins. Orange bitters are there to play the roll that bitters always plays in cocktails, to be the accent which blends and enlivens the flavors.

This recipe calls for the drink to be stirred as opposed to shaken. Shaking this drink will result in a cloudy mess while stirring it will give you a crystal clear liquid to pour into a glass.

As for the garnish, on a sweet Martini you can also use a cherry if you wish, and on a dry Martini olives are acceptable, but my preference is to serve them on the side instead.

Manhattan

- 2¼ ounces (67ml) American rye or bourbon whiskey
- ¾ ounce (22ml) sweet vermouth
- Dash Angostura bitters

Stir with ice.

Strain into a cocktail glass.

Garnish with a cherry.

Similarities between the Manhattan and the Martini are obvious. Spirit, vermouth, bitters: a simple combination, and one that is elegant and refined as well as bold and assertive.

Like the Martini, a Manhattan is traditionally made with sweet vermouth, and if you wanted it to be made with dry instead, you'd ask for a dry Manhattan. Vermouth cocktails can also be *perfect*, meaning they are made from equal amounts of sweet and dry vermouth. This is a variation worth trying as you acquaint yourself with the Manhattan and the Martini.

It should come as no surprise that the Manhattan almost certainly originated in New York City. More precise details, however, are difficult to nail down. The first recorded appearances are in the early 1880s, and many accounts indicate that it was created for a banquet hosted by Jennie Jerome, Winston Churchill's mother, at the Manhattan Club. The banquet celebrated Samuel Tilden's election as governor. The story doesn't hold up, however, since the inaugural celebrations coincided with the precise time Jennie Jerome was giving birth to her famous son in Oxfordshire, England.

The traditional Martini suffered terribly following Prohibition, but the Manhattan wasn't inflicted with a similar fate. You may occasionally encounter a bartender who will leave out the bitters, but, for the most part, the recipe is intact and the drink recognizable. The worst, and very common, offense is that bartenders will shake their Manhattans instead of stirring them. This not only results in a cloudy drink but unappetizing debris of foam across the top. Like a Martini, the Manhattan should always be stirred.

Bloody Mary

- 1½ ounce (45ml) vodka
- 3 ounces (90ml) tomato juice
- ½ ounce (15ml) lemon juice
- Worcestershire sauce to taste
- Tabasco sauce to taste
- Black pepper to taste
- Celery salt to taste

Roll with ice until properly chilled, and then pour into a tall glass.

Garnish with a celery stalk and a wedge of lemon.

Let's start off by defining what *roll* means. Using a normal Boston Shaker, pour the ingredients from the mixing tin to the mixing glass and back again. This will mix and chill the ingredients well without causing the tomato juice to break down and get thin. You could also shake the ingredients very gently or stir them, but rolling is a fun change of pace.

It's said that George Jessel came up with a drink combining equal parts vodka and tomato juice and called it a Bloody Mary. However, around 1920, Fernand "Pete" Petiot of Harry's New York Bar in Paris turned Jessel's drink into the drink we know today by adding salt, pepper and Worcestershire sauce.

When Prohibition ended, the St. Regis Hotel in New York hired Fernand away from Harry's in Paris, and he brought his Bloody Mary with him. Two changes were made to it, however. Since vodka wasn't widely available in the U.S., gin was used instead. Also, the owners of the St. Regis thought Bloody Mary was too crude of a name, so they renamed it the Red Snapper.

The Bloody Mary is a drink that demands a personalized recipe from one bar to the next. It can be considered the meatloaf of cocktails, since a variety of different flavors and ingredients can be combined together. As long as you keep within broad generalities, everybody still accepts it as meatloaf or, in this case, a Bloody Mary.

Many people like to add to, or replace, the Tabasco sauce with horseradish or wasabi. You can also use any one of hundreds of hot sauces available. For a little extra depth, I like to add a tablespoon of chili powder (dried chilies ground to a powder). Various other seasoning options are almost limitless.

Garnishes also allow variety and creativity. Pickled string beans, asparagus spears, olives, scallions or shrimp are just a few ideas you can use.

Mai Tai

- 1 ounce (30ml) light rum
- 1 ounce (30ml) gold rum
- ½ ounce (15ml) orange curaçao
- ½ ounce (15ml) orgeat (almond syrup)
- ½ ounce (15ml) lime juice
- ½ ounce (15ml) dark rum (optional)

Shake all but the dark rum with ice.

Strain into an ice-filled rocks glass.

Top with the dark rum if you wish, then garnish with a maraschino cherry.

The Mai Tai is the most well known drink to come out of the Tiki era, which started in the 1930s and then began to run out of steam in the 1970s.

At the beginning of the Tiki era, there was an enforced veil of secrecy wrapped around most of the exotic drinks served at Polynesian-inspired restaurants. Because these restaurants wanted to keep these drinks unique to their venue, they guarded their recipes as if they were the crown jewels, which in some respect they were. Secrecy went to such an extreme that even the bartenders didn't know the actual recipes they were making. Recipes would list, for example, "½ ounce syrup #2," without a clue as to what the ingredient really was.

This was, of course, a problem for the consumer. After enjoying a wonderful drink like the Mai Tai at Trader Vic's, he or she might ask for a Mai Tai at another restaurant. The bartender, of course, wouldn't know what it was. But a shrewd bartender might ask the customer a few questions about the drink to see if he or she could approximate it. If the result met with the customer's approval, the recipe would be used to satisfy other requests. This has left us with some recipes listing pineapple juice, grenadine, falernum, orange juice or various other ingredients that should never be used making this drink.

The Mai Tai was invented in 1944 by Victor "Trader Vic" Bergeron. He mixed Jamaican rum, juice from a fresh lime, a few dashes of orange curaçao syrup, some French orgeat and rock candy syrup. According to Trader Vic history, the drink was served to some friends from Tahiti, who promptly proclaimed "*Mai Tai, Roa Ae!*" which in Tahitian means "Out of this world, the best!"

The Recipes

INTRODUCTION

This section contains a very personal collection of recipes that I think you will enjoy. The intent is not to list every conceivable drink recipe but rather represent the best a cocktail or mixed drink has to offer.

Where appropriate, I've included additional information to help you better understand how to make a drink. Sometimes the information will convey the history surrounding a particular drink.

Some of the drinks included have been created by myself or other bartenders around the world, and so you may not be familiar with them. In those cases I've listed who created the drink, when, and usually a comment from the originator providing details on his or her inspiration.

As you read through these recipes, keep in mind that none of them should be seen as the definitive recipe for that drink, just the recipe that I feel represents how its ingredients can be best combined for maximum flavor. You will certainly encounter other recipes for the same drink, which will vary slightly from what you find here. In such cases it can be highly

Old fashioned barware

educational to try the other recipes to discover which variation you prefer.

The specific measurements are recommendations, and you should feel free to adjust the amounts to suit your needs and taste. The important thing to remember is to keep the ratios of the ingredients the same so that the cocktail you mix is the same as the recipe intends.

A FEW QUICK POINTERS TO REMEMBER AS YOU MIX YOUR DRINKS:

- Always strive to use fresh juices.

- Measure everything carefully.

- When cutting a citrus twist, do so over the drink to allow some of the oils to drip into the drink.

- Always use plenty of ice.

- Shake or stir the drink long enough to get it as cold as possible.

The Drinks

Agavoni

(by Bastian Heuser, for Mixology Magazine, Berlin, Germany)

- ¾ ounce (22ml) silver tequila
- ¾ ounce (22ml) Campari
- ¾ ounce (22ml) sweet vermouth
- 2 dashes orange bitters

Add to an ice-filled Delmonico glass and stir to chill and mix.

Garnish with a twist of grapefruit.

Bastian recommends using Tapatio Blanco tequila, Carpano Antica vermouth and The Bitter Truth orange bitters.

"This drink was inspired by the magazine's slogan, '2008:Year of Tequila'. While writing an article about the Margarita I got a bit thirsty and thought of I'd enjoy a Negroni. I was standing behind our office-bar when it hit me to substitute tequila for the gin...and history was written."

-Bastian Heuser

Alexander

- 1½ ounce (45ml) brandy
- 1 ounce (30ml) cream
- 1 ounce (30ml) crème de cacao (brown)

Shake with ice and strain into a cocktail glass.

Garnish with a sprinkle of nutmeg.

This drink is often referred to as a Brandy Alexander which suggests you could use other spirits in place of brandy. A modern interpretation of this drink is known as a Chocolate Martini. If you're ever asked for this, try serving an Alexander and let folks know that is the original version.

Alaska

- 2 ounces (60ml) gin
- ¼ ounce (7ml) Chartreuse
- Dash orange bitters

Stir with ice and strain into a cocktail glass.

Garnish with a twist of lemon peel.

Alexander

Algonquin

- 2 ounces (60ml) rye whiskey
- 1 ounce (30ml) dry vermouth
- 1 ounce (30ml) pineapple juice

Shake with ice and strain into a cocktail glass.

Garnish with a cherry.

This cocktail was named after the Algonquin Hotel, which opened its doors in 1902 in one of New York's most fashionable neighborhoods. The hotel gained its greatest fame a few years later as the home of the Algonquin Round Table, the floating literary lunch at which Alexander Woollcott, Harpo Marx, Dorothy Parker, Robert Benchley and their compatriots held sway on New York's cultural scene. There were in fact several drinks named after this historic venue, but this recipe is the one currently served by the hotel's bartenders.

Americano

- 1 ounce (30ml) Campari
- 1 ounce (30ml) sweet vermouth
- Club soda

Pour Campari and sweet vermouth into highball glass filled with ice and stir.

Top with club soda and garnish with an orange wedge or twist of lemon.

Añejo MANhattan

(by Ryan Magarian)

- 2 ounces (60ml) tequila
- ½ ounce (15ml) sweet vermouth
- ¼ ounce (7ml) Licor 43
- 1 dash Angostura bitters
- 1 dash Regan's No. 6 orange bitters

Stir with ice and strain into a cocktail glass.

Ryan recommends using El Tesoro Añejo Tequila for this drink, and when he makes it he garnishes it with mole salami, which is a salami flavored with various spices, chocolate and cinnamon. Wrap the mole salami around a brandy soaked cherry which has been stuck on a pick.

"The Añejo MANhattan was created to be the masculine half of a his and hers Manhattan menu offering that can be enjoyed at Sofitel Hotel Bars across North America."

-Ryan Magarian

Añejo MANhatttan

Aviation

Ante

- 1¾ ounce (52ml) calvados or apple brandy
- ¾ ounce (22ml) Dubonnet
- ½ ounce (15ml) Cointreau
- 1 dash Angostura bitters

Stir with ice and strain into a cocktail glass.

Aviation

- 2 ounces (60ml) gin
- ½ ounce (15ml) maraschino liqueur
- ¼ ounce (7ml) lemon juice

Shake with ice and strain into a cocktail glass.

Garnish with a cherry.

The first recorded version of this recipe was by Hugo Ensslin in *Recipes for Mixed Drinks* published in 1916. That version included a dash of crème de violette, which would have tinted the drink a light sky blue. When the recipe was reprinted in Harry Craddock's *The Savoy Cocktail Book*, the crème de violette was omitted, and it's been absent ever since. Crème de violette is currently hard to find, but it makes an excellent addition to this drink if you come across it.

Bacardi Cocktail

- 2 ounces (60ml) light Bacardi rum
- 1 ounce (30ml) lemon or lime juice
- 2 dashes grenadine syrup

Shake with ice and strain into a cocktail glass.

Although it existed before, this drink became quite popular after Prohibition. Although the recipe calls for Bacardi rum, many establishments used whatever rum they happened to have on hand. Eventually the Bacardi Company decided enough was enough and took the matter to court in 1936. New York State sided with Bacardi and ruled that in order to be called a Bacardi Cocktail, the drink must always be made with Bacardi rum.

1930s

Bamboo

- 1½ ounce (45ml) dry vermouth
- 1½ ounce (45ml) dry sherry
- 1 dash Angostura bitters
- 1 dash orange bitters

Stir with ice and strain into a cocktail glass.

Garnish with an orange twist.

There are several accounts of the origins of this name. One claims the name comes from Bob Cole's 1902 hit song *Under the Bamboo Tree*, but William Boothby, a noted bartender of the day, says in his 1908 book *The World's Drinks* that the drink was created and named by Louis Eppinger, Yokohama, Japan.

Beach Blanket

(by Francesco Lafranconi, for the Hard Rock Cafe Steakhouse, Tampa, Florida)

- 1 ounce (30ml) Jägermeister
- 1 ounce (30ml) coffee liqueur
- 1 ounce (30ml) raspberry liqueur
- 1 ounce (30ml) heavy whipping cream

Shake the Jägermeister, coffee liqueur and raspberry liqueurs with ice.

Strain into a cocktail glass.

Float the whipping cream on the top.

Garnish with a pinch of cinnamon-sugar.

"Think young people, a bonfire on the beach...jäger shots...and a creamy spice character with coffee and raspberry flavors...yummy..."

-Francesco Lafranconi

Bellini

- 1 ounce (30ml) white peach purée
- 5 ounces (150ml) sparkling wine (Italian Prosecco)

Pour peach purée into a champagne flute and add sparkling wine.

To be authentic, the peach purée should be made from fresh white peaches which have been peeled and then squeezed to release their juices. Or you can use a commercial white peach purée made by a company such as Perfect Purée of Napa Valley.

Bijou

Bermuda Rum Swizzle

- 2 ounces (60ml) dark rum
- 1 ounce (30ml) lime juice
- 1 ounce (30ml) pineapple juice
- 1 ounce (30ml) orange juice
- ¼ ounce (7ml) falernum

Shake with ice and strain into an ice-filled highball or Collins glass.

Garnish with a slice of orange and a cherry.

This is a popular drink in bars and restaurants in Bermuda. Many travelers come back from Bermuda looking for a recipe only to discover that falernum is rather hard to find here. Fortunately that is beginning to change, and a few different brands are now available.

To make this as a true swizzle, use a traditional swizzle stick to mix and froth the drink.

Between The Sheets

- 1 ounce (30ml) brandy
- 1 ounce (30ml) light rum
- 1 ounce (30ml) Cointreau
- ½ ounce (15ml) lemon juice

Shake with ice and strain into a cocktail glass.

Garnish with a twist of lemon.

An obvious variation of the Sidecar and Daiquiri, this drink appears to have been a European cocktail created during Prohibition. It's interesting because it's one of the few cocktails that use two base spirits.

Bijou

- 1 ounce (30ml) gin
- 1 ounce (30ml) green Chartreuse
- 1 ounce (30ml) sweet vermouth
- 1 dash orange bitters

Stir with ice and strain into a cocktail glass.

Garnish with a cherry and a lemon twist.

In French, bijou means "jewel," and so I prefer the dual garnish of a cherry and tightly curled spiral of lemon twist in the bottom of the glass. It almost looks like art.

Bistro Sidecar

(Created by Kathy Casey, Kathy Casey Food Studios, Ballard, Washington)

- 1½ ounce (45ml) brandy
- ½ ounce (15ml) Tuaca
- ½ ounce (15ml) Frangelico
- ¼ ounce (7ml) of lemon juice
- ¼ ounce (7ml) of simple syrup
- Wedge of tangerine, squeezed

Shake with ice and strain into a sugar-rimmed cocktail glass.

Garnish with a roasted hazelnut.

Black Feather

(Created by Robert Hess, 2000)

- 2 ounces (60ml) brandy
- 1 ounce (30ml) dry vermouth
- ½ ounce (15ml) Cointreau
- 1 dash of bitters

Stir with ice and strain into a cocktail glass.

Garnish with a lemon twist.

I specifically created this drink to be the house cocktail for my home bar which I've nicknamed the Black Feather. In my original recipe I used my own homemade bitters, but, lacking that, Angostura works just fine.

Black Russian

Black Russian

- 2 ounces (60ml) vodka
- 1 ounce (30ml) coffee liqueur

Pour over ice into a rocks glass.

Blackberry Fizz

(by Jonathan Pogash, for Madison and Vine Wine Bar and American Bistro in New York)

- ¾ ounce (22ml) gin
- ¾ ounce (22ml) Lillet Blanc
- 3 fresh blackberries
- ¼ ounce (7ml) lemon juice
- ¼ ounce (7ml) simple syrup
- 3 ounces (90ml) champagne

Muddle the blackberries in the lemon juice and simple syrup.

Add the gin and Lillet and shake with ice, then strain into a flute glass.

Top with champagne and garnish with a fresh blackberry.

Jonathan recommends using Bombay Sapphire for the gin and Moët & Chandon for the champagne.

"In this drink, I wanted to combine fresh fruit flavors with several varieties of wines – those being the Lillet and champagne. The gin really adds spice and marries the fruit with the wine."

— Jonathan Pogash

Blackstar

(by Jim Meehan, for PDT in New York)

- 2 ounces (60ml) vodka
- ¾ ounce (22ml) lime juice
- ¾ ounce (22ml) grapefruit juice
- ¼ ounce (7ml) simple syrup
- ¼ ounce (7ml) sambuca
- 1 whole star anise pod (for garnish)

Shake with ice and strain into a cocktail glass.

Garnish by floating the star anise pod in the center.

Jim recommends using Luxardo or Borsci sambuca for this drink.

Blood and Sand

- ¾ ounce (22ml) Scotch whisky
- ¾ ounce (22ml) Cherry Heering
- ¾ ounce (22ml) sweet vermouth
- ¾ ounce (22ml) orange juice

Shake with ice and strain into a cocktail glass.

With so few Scotch based cocktails, I'm always on the lookout for ones to add to my collection. This is a fairly old one. It was named for the 1922 Rudolph Valentino silent movie.

Bloody Mary

- 1½ ounce (45ml) vodka
- 3 ounces (90ml) tomato juice
- ½ ounce (15ml) lemon juice
- Worcestershire sauce to taste
- Tabasco sauce to taste
- Black pepper to taste
- Celery salt to taste

Roll with ice until properly chilled, and then pour into a tall glass.

Garnish with a celery stalk and a wedge of lemon.

Please exercise creativity with this drink and experiment with other ways to enhance its savory nature.

Bloody Mary

Bloomsbury

(Created by Robert Hess, 2003)

- 2 ounces (60ml) gin
- ½ ounce (15ml) Licor 43
- ½ ounce (15ml) Lillet Blanc
- 2 dashes Peychaud's bitters

Stir with ice and strain into a cocktail glass.

Garnish with lemon twist.

I created this drink as part of a promotion for Tanqueray 10, and so that is the recommended gin to use. The name comes from the fact that Tanqueray originated in the Bloomsbury district of London.

Bobbo's Bride

(Created by Laurel Semmes, 1999)

- 1 ounce (30ml) gin
- 1 ounce (30ml) vodka
- ½ ounce (15ml) peach liqueur
- ¼ ounce (7ml) Campari

Stir with ice and strain into a cocktail glass.

Garnish with a slice of fresh peach.

Bobby Burns

- 1½ ounce (45ml) blended scotch whisky
- 1½ ounce (45ml) sweet vermouth
- ¼ ounce (7ml) Bénédictine

Stir with ice and strain into a cocktail glass.

Garnish with a lemon twist.

Named after the venerable Scottish poet Robert Burns, this cocktail apparently made its first appearance shortly before Prohibition. Unfortunately it only occasionally shows up today. Some recipes prefer to use Drambuie instead of Bénédictine, probably because Drambuie is a scotch-based liqueur and so completes the story a little better.

Bordeaux Cocktail

(Created by Tito Class for Mona's Bistro & Lounge, Seattle)

- 2¼ ounces (67ml) citrus vodka
- ¾ ounce (22ml) Lillet Blanc

Stir with ice and strain into a cocktail glass.

Garnish with a lemon twist.

Bourbon Crusta

(By Gary & Mardee Regan, The Book of Bourbon*)*

- 2 ounces (60ml) bourbon whiskey
- ½ ounce (15ml) tripe sec
- ½ ounce (15ml) maraschino liqueur
- ½ ounce (15ml) lemon juice
- 2 dashes orange bitters

Shake with ice and strain into a sugar rimmed cocktail glass.

Garnish with an orange peel.

A bourbon based variation of the Crusta, a once popular drink style in New Orleans.

Brandy Cobbler

- Large chunk of pineapple
- Orange wedge
- Lemon wedge
- ¾ ounce (22ml) raspberry syrup or raspberry liqueur
- 1 ounce (30ml) water
- 2 ounces (60ml) brandy

Muddle the pineapple, orange, and lemon with the raspberry syrup and water in a mixing glass.

Add the brandy and shake with ice.

Strain into a large wine goblet filled with crushed ice.

Garnish with lemon, orange, pineapple and fresh raspberries.

Brandy Crusta

- 1½ ounce (45ml) brandy
- ¼ ounce (7ml) maraschino liqueur
- ¼ ounce (7ml) Cointreau
- ¼ ounce (7ml) lemon juice

Shake with ice and strain into a small sugar rimmed wine glass.

Garnish with a long wide spiral of lemon peel.

Jerry Thomas wrote about the Crusta in his 1862 *The Bar-tender's Guide or How to Mix All Kinds of Plain and Fancy Drinks:*

"The Crusta is an improvement on the 'Cocktail' and is said to have been invented by Santina, a celebrated Spanish caterer."

1938

RECIPES

Bourbon Crusta

Brandy Shrub

(will make 3 cups, enough for 12 drinks)

- 2 cups (500ml) brandy
- 1 whole lemon
- 1 cup (225g) sugar
- 1 cup (250ml) water
- ⅔ cup (160ml) sherry

Peel the rind off of the lemon, and then juice it.

Place the rind, juice, and brandy in a jar, then seal and store in a cool dark place for three days, and then strain.

Then make simple syrup by simmering the water, and stirring in the sugar until dissolved. Allow this to cool, then add it to the brandy/lemon mixture, and then add the sherry. Bottle and store in the refrigerator.

To make a drink, place 2 ounces (60ml) of the mixture into an ice-filled highball glass, then top with club soda.

Brandy Smash

- 2 ounces (60ml) brandy
- ½ ounce (15ml) simple syrup
- 3 sprigs mint

Add simple syrup and mint to a rocks glass, and muddle lightly to express mint flavors into the syrup.

Fill with crushed ice and then add the brandy.

Stir to chill.

Garnish with a mint sprig.

Serve with straws.

You can make this with any spirit, i.e., a gin smash, rum smash, etc.

Bridal

- 2 ounces (60ml) gin
- 1 ounce (30ml) sweet vermouth
- ¼ ounce (7ml) maraschino liqueur
- Dash orange bitters

Stir with ice and strain into a cocktail glass.

Garnish with a cherry.

Bronx

- •1½ ounce (45ml) gin
- •¾ ounce (22ml) orange juice
- •¼ ounce (7ml) sweet vermouth
- •¼ ounce (7ml) dry vermouth

Shake with ice and strain into a cocktail glass.

Prior to Prohibition, the Bronx was one of *the* cocktails of its day, about as popular as the Cosmopolitan is today. When making the Bronx, be careful with the orange juice. Orange juice has a tendency to become the dominant component, which results in a weak tasting drink.

Brooklyn

- •2¼ ounces (67ml) rye or bourbon whiskey
- •¾ ounce (22ml) sweet vermouth
- •1 dash Amer Picon
- •1 dash maraschino liqueur

Stir with ice and strain into a cocktail glass.

Here is the first of a number of Amer Picon recipes you'll find here. These recipes are presented in the hopes that Amer Picon will again be distributed in the U.S.

1930s

Buck's Fizz

- 2 ounces (60ml) orange juice
- 1 dash cherry brandy
- ¼ ounce (7ml) gin
- 4 ounces (120ml) sparkling wine

Slowly pour the ingredients in the order listed into a champagne flute or wine glass. Garnish with an orange wedge.

Apparently invented during the 1920s by the personal barman for Captain Herbert John Buckmaster (known today mainly as the first husband of famed British actress Gladys Cooper), this drink is considered to be the precursor to the Mimosa. Many recipes for a Buck's Fizz will incorrectly refer to it as identical to the Mimosa. The version here is the original recipe.

Bull Shot

- 1½ ounce (45ml) vodka
- 3 ounces (90ml) beef bouillon
- ¼ ounce (7ml) lemon juice
- Worcestershire sauce to taste
- Tabasco sauce to taste
- Black pepper to taste
- Celery salt to taste

Shake with ice and strain into an ice-filled highball glass.

Garnish with some cracked black pepper and a wedge of lime.

This is essentially a Bloody Mary using beef bouillon instead of tomato juice. You may have to adjust your seasoning if you're using a pre-seasoned bouillon.

Cabaret

- 1½ ounce (45ml) gin
- 1 ounce (30ml) dry vermouth
- ¼ ounce (7ml) Bénédictine
- 2 dashes Angostura bitters

Stir with ice and strain into a cocktail glass.

Garnish with a cherry.

1937

Cable Car

(by Tony Abou-Ganim, for the Starlight Room in San Francisco, 1993)

- 1½ ounce (45ml) spiced rum
- ¾ ounce (22ml) orange curaçao
- 1 ounce (30ml) lemon juice
- ½ ounce (15ml) simple syrup

Shake with ice and then strain into a cocktail glass which has been rimmed with a cinnamon sugar mixture.

Garnish with an orange twist.

Tony recommends making this drink with Captain Morgan's Spiced Rum and Marie Brizard orange curaçao.

"This drink's name comes from the geography of its house of origin …One of the city's landmark properties, the Sir Francis Drake Hotel, is located along the world famous Nob Hill cable car tracks. Its Starlight Room is affectionately referred to as the lounge that can be found 'between the stars and the cable cars.' "

-Tony Abou-Ganim

Caesar

- 1 ounce (30ml) vodka
- 4 ounces (120ml) tomato-clam juice (a.k.a. Clamato juice)
- Pinch of salt and pepper
- Dash Worcestershire sauce
- 2 to 3 dashes horseradish
- Celery salt
- Celery stalk

Shake ingredients with ice.

Coat rim of a highball or Delmonico glass with celery salt, and then fill with ice.

Strain mixture into glass.

Garnish with a celery stalk and a lemon wedge.

This is clearly a variation of the Bloody Mary. The primary difference is that Clamato juice replaces plain tomato juice. This version is very popular in Canada.

Calvados Cocktail

- 1½ ounce (45ml) calvados (apple brandy)
- 1½ ounce (45ml) orange juice
- ¾ ounce (22ml) Cointreau
- ¾ ounce (22ml) orange bitters

Shake with ice and then strain into a cocktail glass.

Calvados is an apple brandy made in the Normandy region of France. In America, it is called Applejack.

Caipirinha

- 2 ounces (60ml) cachaça (Brazilian white rum)
- 1 teaspoon (5ml) sugar
- 1 lime

Wash the lime, and cut it into quarters.

Put limes and sugar into a tumbler, and muddle hard.

Add the cachaça and stir.

Fill with ice, and stir again.

I like to use granulated sugar instead of simple syrup for this drink to allow the sugar to help grind out some of the flavorful oils from the lime's skin.

The Caipirinha is a popular drink in Brazil where cachaça, distilled from sugar cane, comes from. Not too long ago, cachaça was extremely hard to find, but today it is relatively common, and, with its availability, Caipirinha has grown in popularity.

Caipirinha

Canton

- 2 ounces (60ml) Jamaican rum
- ½ ounce (15ml) maraschino liqueur
- ½ ounce (15ml) orange curaçao
- 1 dash grenadine

Stir with ice and then strain into a cocktail glass.

Garnish with a cherry and orange twist.

Captain's Blood

- 2 ounces (60ml) dark rum
- ½ ounce (15ml) lime juice
- ½ ounce (15ml) simple syrup
- 2 dashes Angostura bitters

Shake with ice and then strain into a cocktail glass.

Garnish with a spiral of lemon peel.

Caprice

- 1½ ounce (45ml) gin
- ½ ounce (15ml) dry vermouth
- ½ ounce (15ml) Bénédictine
- 1 dash orange bitters

Stir with ice and then strain into a cocktail glass.

Casino

- 2 ounces (60ml) gin
- ⅛ ounce (4ml) lemon juice
- ⅛ ounce (4ml) maraschino liqueur
- 2 dashes orange bitters

Shake with ice and then strain into a cocktail glass.

Garnish with a cherry.

Champagne Antoine

(Created by Robert Hess, for Antoine's Restaurant, New Orleans)

- 1 ounce (30ml) gin
- 1 ounce (30ml) dry vermouth
- ⅛ ounce (4ml) Pernod
- 4 ounces (120ml) dry champagne

Shake the gin, vermouth, and Pernod with ice and then strain into a champagne flute.

Top with champagne and garnish with a lemon twist.

Inspired by a dinner at New Orleans' famous Antoine restaurant, I created this drink as part of the annual *Tales of the Cocktail* event there.

Champagne Cocktail

- 6 ounces (180ml) chilled champagne
- 1 sugar cube (1 teaspoon/5ml)
- Angostura bitters

Soak sugar cube with Angostura bitters and then drop the sugar cube into a flute glass filled with champagne.

Garnish with a lemon twist.

Champagne Flamingo

- ¾ ounce (22ml) vodka
- ¾ ounce (22ml) Campari
- 5 ounces (150ml) chilled champagne

Shake vodka and Campari with ice and then strain into a flute glass.

Top with champagne and then garnish with an orange twist.

Champs Elysées

- 1 ounce (30ml) brandy (cognac)
- ¼ ounce (7ml) green Chartreuse
- 1 ounce (30ml) lemon juice
- 1 dash Angostura bitters

Shake with ice and strain into a cocktail glass.

Garnish with a lemon twist.

Chaplin

- ¾ ounce (22ml) bourbon whiskey
- ¾ ounce (22ml) dry sherry
- ¾ ounce (22ml) Ramazzotti
- ⅛ ounce (4ml) Cointreau
- 2 dashes orange bitters

Stir with ice and then strain into a cocktail glass.

Garnish with a lemon twist.

Ramazzotti is an Italian bitter digestif wine with a noted orange flavor. It can be relatively hard to find.

Chas

(By Murray Stenson, for the Zig Zag Café, Seattle)

- 2¼ ounces (67ml) bourbon whiskey
- ¼ ounce (7ml) amaretto
- ¼ ounce (7ml) Bénédictine
- ¼ ounce (7ml) Cointreau
- ¼ ounce (7ml) orange curaçao

Stir with ice and strain into a cocktail glass.

Garnish with an orange twist.

This drink was created on the spur of the moment for a customer named Charles. Charles, who loves bourbon, challenged the bartender to make him something "new."

Clover Club

Chrysanthemum Cocktail

- 2 ounces (60ml) dry vermouth
- 1 ounce (30ml) Bénédictine
- 3 dashes absinthe or pastis

Stir with ice and strain into a cocktail glass.

Garnish with a twist of orange

Cloister

- 1½ ounce (45ml) gin
- ½ ounce (15ml) yellow Chartreuse
- ½ ounce (15ml) grapefruit juice
- ¼ ounce (7ml) lemon juice
- ¼ ounce (7ml) simple syrup

Shake with ice and strain into a cocktail glass.

Garnish with a grapefruit twist.

If you can't find yellow Chartreuse, you can use the normal green version. Since the flavor of the green is more intense, remember to use a little less of it.

Clover Club

- 1½ ounce (45ml) gin
- ¼ ounce (7ml) grenadine
- ¾ ounce (22ml) lemon juice
- 1 egg white

First shake this without any ice to help foam the egg, then add ice to the shaker and shake to chill.

Strain into a fancy cocktail or wine glass.

With the addition of mint leaves before shaking, this becomes a Clover Leaf Cocktail. The Clover Club made its appearance right before Prohibition and was an extremely popular cocktail in its day.

Coffee Cocktail

- 1½ ounce (45ml) port
- 1½ ounce (45ml) brandy
- 1 teaspoon (5ml) simple syrup
- 1 whole egg

Shake hard with ice and strain into a wine glass.

Garnish with grated nutmeg.

Properly labeled, this drink is a flip rather than a cocktail. The 1887 edition of Jerry Thomas's *Bartenders' Guide* mentioned this confusion and pointed out that, in this case, the label cocktail was misleading since the drink didn't include coffee or bitters. However, when properly made, it does look like a cup of coffee with foamed milk.

1950s

Coffee Nudge

- ½ ounce (15ml) brandy
- ½ ounce (15ml) coffee liqueur
- ½ ounce (15ml) dark crème de cacao
- 5 ounces (150ml) coffee

Whip cream for garnish.

In a pre-warmed coffee mug, add the brandy, coffee liqueur and crème de cacao.

Pour in the coffee (decaf can be used if desired) and top with a dollop of whip cream.

Serve with cocktail straws.

In some parts of the country, this drink is referred to as the Keoke Coffee.

Commodore

- 2 ounces (60ml) bourbon whiskey
- ¾ ounce (22ml) white crème de cacao
- ½ ounce (15ml) lemon juice
- 1 dash grenadine

Shake with ice and strain into champagne flute.

Companero

(by Sean Muldoon, for the Merchant Hotel, Belfast, Northern Ireland)

- 1 ounce (30ml) rum
- ½ ounce (15ml) white crème de cacao
- ½ ounce (15ml) lime juice
- 3 torn basil leaves
- ¼ ounce (7ml) sugar syrup

Shake with ice and double-strain into a cocktail glass.

Garnish with a lime wedge.

Sean recommends using an aged Cuban rum.

"I had read that basil and lime had a natural affinity to chocolate ice-cream, and so thought about doing what could be considered a variation of the Daiquiri which added both crème de cacao and fresh basil. I then named this after the Spanish word for comrade."

       - Sean Muldoon

Corleone

(by Ryan Magarian)

- 5 white grapes
- 1½ ounce (45ml) gin
- ½ ounce (15ml) grappa
- ½ ounce (15ml) lemon juice
- ¾ ounce (22ml) simple syrup
- 1 dash orange bitters

Muddle the grapes in a mixing glass, then add everything else and shake with ice.

Strain into a cocktail glass.

Garnish with a single white grape sliced midway and resting on the glass rim.

"I created this drink as an attempt to encapsulate the flavor of a liquefied Sicilian countryside."   -Ryan Magarian

Corleone

Corpse Reviver #1

- 2 ounces (60ml) brandy (cognac)
- 1 ounce (30ml) sweet vermouth
- 1 ounce (30ml) applejack

Stir with ice and strain into a cocktail glass.

Corpse Revivers were a style of drink specifically intended for a bit of the hair of the dog (an expression that refers to alcohol used as a treatment for a hangover). Hard to say exactly what it was about these drinks that made them seem more appropriate for this use than other drinks.

Corpse Reviver #2

- ¾ ounce (22ml) gin
- ¾ ounce (22ml) lemon juice
- ¾ ounce (22ml) Cointreau
- ¾ ounce (22ml) Lillet Blanc
- Dash absinthe or pastis

Shake with ice and strain into a cocktail glass.

This is the Corpse Reviver that has best stood the test of time.

Corpse Reviver #3

- 1 ounce (30ml) brandy (cognac)
- 1 ounce (30ml) Campari
- 1 ounce (30ml) triple sec
- ½ ounce (15ml) lemon juice

Shake with ice and strain into a cocktail glass.

This third variation on the Corpse Reviver is for good measure.

Cosmopolitan

- 1½ ounce (45ml) citrus vodka
- ½ ounce (15ml) Cointreau
- 1 ounce (30ml) cranberry juice
- ¾ ounce (22ml) lime juice

Shake with ice and strain into a cocktail glass.

Garnish with lime wedge.

Often maligned, probably because it is frequently made with sour mix or other time/cost cutting measures. If you take the time to make this drink properly, you'll agree it deserves its long-held popularity.

Country Gentleman

- 1½ ounce (45ml) apple brandy
- ¾ ounce (22ml) orange curaçao
- ¼ ounce (7ml) lemon juice
- 1 teaspoon (5ml) simple syrup

Shake with ice and strain into cocktail glass.

Garnish with a lemon twist.

Crux

- ¾ ounce (22ml) brandy
- ¾ ounce (22ml) Dubonnet
- ¾ ounce (22ml) Cointreau
- ¾ ounce (22ml) lemon juice

Stir with ice and strain into a cocktail glass.

Cuba Libre

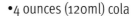

- 2 ounces (60ml) rum
- 4 ounces (120ml) cola
- Lime wedge

Pour into an ice-filled tumbler.

Add a generous squeeze of lime, and then add the rind as a garnish.

Almost a Rum & Coke. However, when properly made, a Cuba Libre will include a squeeze of lime while a Rum & Coke is just garnished with a lime wedge.

Some accounts indicate that the original Cuba Libre also included gin and Angostura bitters.

Daiquiri

- 2 ounces (60ml) light rum
- ¾ ounce (22ml) simple syrup
- ½ ounce (15ml) lime juice

Shake with ice and strain into a cocktail glass.

Garnish with a lime slice.

Blended daiquiris are popular among younger drinkers, but, to really appreciate this drink, you should try this original recipe.

Cuba Libre

Dark 'n Stormy

- 2 ounces (60ml) Gosling's Black Seal rum
- 4 ounces (120ml) ginger beer

Pour into an ice-filled highball glass.

Garnish with a lime wedge.

Recipes can't be trademarked, but names can. The Dark 'n Stormy is trademarked by Gosling Brothers, so this drink is always made with Gosling's Black Seal rum.

Death in the Afternoon

- 1 ounce (30ml) absinthe or pastis
- 5 ounces (150ml) chilled sparkling wine

Pour absinthe or pastis into a champagne flute and then top with sparkling wine.

Delilah

- 1½ ounce (45ml) gin
- ¾ ounce (22ml) Cointreau
- ¾ ounce (22ml) lemon juice

Shake with ice and strain into a cocktail glass.

Delmonico

- 1 ounce (30ml) gin
- ½ ounce (15ml) brandy
- ½ ounce (15ml) dry vermouth
- ½ ounce (15ml) sweet vermouth
- 1 dash orange bitters

Stir with ice and strain into a cocktail glass.

Garnish with a lemon twist.

Dark 'n Stormy

Derby

- 2 ounces (60ml) bourbon whiskey
- ¼ ounce (7ml) Bénédictine
- 1 dash Angostura bitters

Stir with ice and strain into a cocktail glass.

Garnish with a lemon peel.

Deshler

- 1½ ounce (45ml) rye whiskey
- 1 ounce (30ml) Dubonnet rouge
- ¼ ounce (7ml) Cointreau
- 2 dashes Peychaud's bitters
- 1 orange twist (in mixing glass)
- 1 lemon twist (in mixing glass)

Stir with ice and strain into a cocktail glass.

Garnish with an orange peel.

Diablo

- 1½ ounce (45ml) tequila
- ¾ ounce (22ml) crème de cassis
- ½ ounce (15ml) lime juice
- Ginger ale

Shake tequila, cassis, and lime juice with ice and strain into a Collins glass.

Top with ginger ale and garnish with a lime wheel.

Diabolo

- 2 ounces (60ml) rum
- ½ ounce (15ml) Cointreau
- ½ ounce (15ml) dry vermouth
- 2 dashes Angostura bitters

Stir with ice and strain into a cocktail glass.

Garnish with a twist of orange peel.

East India House

- 1¾ ounce (52ml) brandy
- ¼ ounce (7ml) rum
- ¼ ounce (7ml) pineapple juice
- ¼ ounce (7ml) orange curaçao
- 1 dash orange bitters

Shake with ice.

Strain into a cocktail glass.

Garnish with a lemon twist and cherry.

This excellent cocktail is also known as the East India Cocktail. It first appeared in a slightly different form in Harry Johnson's 1882 *Bartenders' Manual*, which is now extremely rare. By the time Harry Craddock published his *Savoy Cocktail Book* in 1930, the recipe evolved to the form shown here.

Eastern Sour

(by Victor "Trader Vic" Bergeron)

- •2 ounces (60ml) bourbon whiskey
- •1½ ounce (45ml) orange juice
- •1 ounce (30ml) lime juice
- •¼ ounce (7ml) orgeat (almond syrup)
- •¼ ounce (7ml) simple syrup

Shake with ice and strain into an ice-filled rocks glass.

Garnish with spent shell of lime.

El Presidente

- •1½ ounce (45ml) white rum
- •½ ounce (15ml) dry vermouth
- •½ ounce (15ml) orange curaçao
- •Dash of grenadine

Stir with ice and strain into a cocktail glass.

Garnish with an orange twist.

Elderthorn

(by Robert Hess, 2007)

- •1 ounce (30ml) cognac or brandy
- •½ ounce (15ml) St. Germain Elder-flower liqueur
- •½ ounce (15ml) Cynar

Stir with ice and strain into a cocktail glass.

Elderflower syrup has been popular in cocktails in the U.K. for many years, but it hasn't been readily available in the U.S. Recently a new Elderflower Liqueur came out, and I just had to try using it in a new cocktail.

1937

Eggnog

(Enough for 6 people)

- 6 eggs
- 1 cup (200g) sugar
- ½ teaspoon (2.5ml) salt
- 1 cup (250ml) golden rum
- 1 pint (475ml) cream
- 1 pint (475ml) milk
- Nutmeg

In a large bowl, beat eggs until light and foamy.

Add sugar and salt, beating until thick and lemon colored.

Stir in rum, cream, and milk.

Chill at least three hours.

Serve with a sprinkle of nutmeg.

If all you've ever had is commercial eggnog from a carton, you really deserve to try the real thing.

Eggnog will keep well in the refrigerator for quite some time. The flavor will improve as it rests, and so it's even better if you make it a day or more before you need it.

Floridita

- 1½ ounce (45ml) rum
- ½ ounce (15ml) lime juice
- ½ ounce (15ml) sweet vermouth
- ⅛ ounce (4ml) white crème de cacao
- ⅛ ounce (4ml) grenadine

Shake with ice and strain into a cocktail glass.

Garnish with a lime twist.

This drink is only one of many which are named after the Floridita bar in Havana, Cuba. When the drink is properly made, the crème de cacao should present just the barest hint of chocolate.

Fallen Leaves

(By Charles Schumann, 1982)

- ¾ ounce (22ml) calvados (apple brandy)
- ¾ ounce (22ml) sweet vermouth
- ¼ ounce (7ml) dry vermouth
- Dash brandy
- Squeeze lemon peel

Stir with ice and strain into a cocktail glass.

Squeeze lemon twist into drink, and use as garnish.

This is a drink which illustrates the importance of the oils of the lemon twist. Without them, this drink just isn't the same.

Floridita

Fancy-Free Cocktail

- 2 ounces (60ml) bourbon whiskey
- ½ ounce (15ml) maraschino liqueur
- 1 dash Angostura bitters
- 1 dash orange bitters

Stir with ice and strain into a cocktail glass.

Fin de Siècle

- 1½ ounce (45ml) gin
- ¾ ounce (22ml) sweet vermouth
- ¼ ounce (7ml) Amer Picon
- 1 dash orange bitters

Stir with ice and strain into a cocktail glass.

Fin de siècle is French for "end of the century."

Fancy-Free

Fish House Punch

(Enough for 32 people)

- 1½ cups (300g) superfine sugar
- 2 quarts (2L) water
- 1 quart (1L) lemon juice
- 2 quarts (2L) dark rum
- 1 quart (1L) brandy (cognac)
- 4 ounces (120ml) peach brandy

In a large punch bowl, combine sugar and about half of the water.

Stir until fully dissolved.

Then add the lemon juice and spirits, then slip in as large of a block of ice as you can. Allow to sit for at least 30 minutes before serving.

Use the reserved water to adjust for balance if necessary.

There are a few different recipes for Fish House Punch and, hopefully, this is one of the most authentic. It originated in Philadelphia, Pennsylvania in 1732, when a gentlemen's club, which eventually turned into an eating establishment, served it as one of their standard libations.

Fog Cutter

(by Victor "Trader Vic" Bergeron, 1950)

- 2 ounces (60ml) lemon juice
- 1 ounce (30ml) orange juice
- ½ ounce (15ml) orgeat (almond syrup)
- 2 ounces (60ml) white rum
- 1 ounce (30ml) brandy
- ½ ounce (15ml) gin
- ½ ounce (15ml) sweet sherry

Shake everything—except sherry—with ice and then pour into tall ice-filled Tiki mug or Collins glass.

Float the sherry over the top.

1950

Frappéed Café Royal

- 1½ ounces (45ml) cognac
- 2 ounces (60ml) espresso

Shake with ice and then strain into a Delmonico glass filled with finely crushed/shaved ice.

Stir with a stirring rod or swizzle stick until well chilled and some ice begins to frost on the outside of the glass.

Top with a little more shaved ice.

Serve with straws.

French 75

- 1 ounce (30ml) gin
- ¼ ounce (7ml) lemon juice
- ⅛ ounce (4ml) simple syrup
- 5 ounces (150ml) champagne

Shake gin, lemon juice and syrup with ice and strain into a flute glass.

Top with champagne.

Named for the 75 millimeter gun used by American forces during World War 1, this drink first appeared in the 1930 *Savoy Cocktail Book* by Harry Craddock.

Some recipes call for brandy instead of gin in the mistaken notion that that's how a French drink should be made. However, the drink isn't French, and gin is the proper spirit to use.

French Quarter

(By Robert Hess, 2004)

- 2½ ounces (75ml) brandy
- ¾ ounce (22ml) Lillet Blanc

Stir with ice and strain into a cocktail glass.

Garnish with a thin quarter wheel of lemon.

Using the Bordeaux cocktail as inspiration, I created this drink specifically to pair with the Trout Almandine served at Antoine's Restaurant in New Orleans.

Frostbite

- 1 ounce (30ml) tequila
- ¾ ounce (22ml) white crème de cacao
- ¾ ounce (22ml) cream

Shake hard with ice to froth the cream a little and strain into a cocktail glass.

Garnish with a sprinkle of nutmeg.

A dash of grenadine turns this drink into a Silk Stocking.

Gibson

- 2½ ounces (75ml) gin
- ½ ounce (15ml) dry vermouth

Stir with ice and strain into a cocktail glass.

Garnish with a cocktail onion.

Essentially a Martini with a different garnish. There are multiple stories about its origin, but none that are a clear winner.

Gibson

Gimlet

- 2¼ ounces (67ml) gin
- ¾ ounce (22ml) Rose's lime juice

Stir with ice and strain into a cocktail glass.

For me, this is the only cocktail which should use Rose's lime juice. Too many bartenders use Rose's as a substitute for fresh lime juice, which it clearly is not.

Gin Buck

- 2 ounces (60ml) gin
- ½ ounce (15ml) lime or lemon juice
- 4 ounces (120ml) ginger ale

Add gin and juice to an ice-filled highball glass, then top with ginger ale.

Stir briefly.

You can make this drink with any base spirit, thus creating a rum buck, tequila buck, etc.

Gin Daisy

- 2½ ounces (75ml) gin
- 1 ounce (30ml) lemon or lime juice
- ½ ounce (15ml) grenadine

Shake with ice and strain into an ice-filled highball glass.

Garnish with a lemon twist.

You can make this drink with any base spirit, thus creating a brandy daisy, rum daisy, etc.

Gin Fix

- 2½ ounces (75ml) gin
- 1 ounce (30ml) lemon or lime juice
- ½ ounce (15ml) pineapple syrup

Shake with ice and strain into an ice-filled Delmonico glass.

Garnish with a lemon twist.

If you can't fine pineapple syrup, you can use ¼ ounce (7ml) pineapple juice and ¼ ounce (7ml) simple syrup.

You can make this drink with any base spirit, thus creating an applejack fix, whiskey fix, etc.

Gin Fizz

- 2 ounces (60ml) gin
- 1 ounce (30ml) lemon juice
- ½ ounce (15ml) simple syrup
- 5 ounces (150ml) club soda

Shake all but the club soda with ice and then strain into an ice-filled Delmonico/fizz glass.

Top with club soda and stir briefly to fizz it up.

If you add a raw egg white before shaking, the drink becomes a silver fizz, with an egg yolk it becomes a golden fizz, and with a whole egg it becomes a royal fizz.

Gin Flip

- 2 ounces (60ml) gin
- ½ ounce (15ml) simple syrup
- 1 whole egg

Shake hard with ice and strain into a Delmonico glass or wine glass.

Garnish with nutmeg.

You can make this drink with any spirit, or with sherry, port, or almost any wine.

Gin Rickey

- 2 ounces (60ml) gin
- ¾ ounce (22ml) lime juice
- ½ ounce (15ml) simple syrup
- 2 ounces (60ml) club soda

Stir all but the club soda in a Collins glass with a couple ice cubes, then top with club soda. Garnish with a lime wedge.

Gin Sling

- 2 ounces (60ml) gin
- ½ ounce (15ml) chilled water
- ½ ounce (15ml) simple syrup

Combine in a rocks glass with a single ice cube.

Stir briefly to combine and serve without straws.

You can make this with any spirit. If desired, you can add a teaspoon of lemon juice.

Gin Tonic Cocktail

(by Sean Muldoon, for the Merchant Hotel, Belfast, Northern Ireland)

- •¾ ounce (22ml) dry gin
- •¾ ounce (22ml) Lillet Blanc
- •¾ ounce (22ml) lime juice
- •½ ounce (15ml) simple syrup
- •2 small sprigs fresh cilantro (coriander leaves)
- •1 dash Peychaud's bitters

Shake with ice and double-strain into a cocktail glass.

Garnish with a lime wedge.

"The goal was to create a fizz-less version of the Gin & Tonic, and serve it as a pre-dinner apéritif. I used Lillet as the replacement for tonic water since it includes quinine, and used coriander because it matches well with the traditional gin botanicals."
- Sean Muldoon, bar manager, The Merchant Hotel

Goat's Delight

- •1¾ ounce (52ml) kirschwasser
- •1¾ ounce (52ml) brandy
- •¼ ounce (7ml) orgeat (almond syrup)
- •¼ ounce (7ml) cream
- •Dash of absinthe or pastis

Shake with ice and strain into a cocktail glass.

Golden Dawn

- •¾ ounce (22ml) gin
- •¾ ounce (22ml) calvados or apple brandy
- •¾ ounce (22ml) apricot brandy
- •¾ ounce (22ml) orange juice

Shake with ice and strain into a cocktail glass.

Golden Dream

- •¾ ounce (22ml) Galliano
- •½ ounce (15ml) Cointreau
- •½ ounce (15ml) orange juice
- •1 tablespoon (15ml) cream

Shake with ice and strain into a cocktail glass.

Galliano

Gotham

(by Robert Hess, 2002)

- ½ teaspoon (2.5ml) absinthe or pastis
- 3 dashes peach bitters
- 2 ounces (60ml) brandy

Coat a chilled small rocks glass with absinthe or pastis, then add the peach bitters and brandy.

Garnish with a lemon twist.

I patterned this drink after the Sazerac, and intended it to be a contemplative drink, one you might sip as you sit in a comfortable chair in front of a fire with your trusty dog curled up at your feet.

The Govenor's

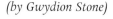

(by Gwydion Stone)

- 1½ ounce (45ml) gin
- 1½ ounce (45ml) Pimm's No. 1
- ½ ounce (15ml) lime juice
- ½ ounce (15ml) simple syrup
- ½ ounce (15ml) absinthe

Shake with ice and strain into a cocktail glass.

Grasshopper

- 1 ounce (30ml) green crème de menthe
- 1 ounce (30ml) white crème de cacao
- 2 ounces (60ml) heavy cream

Shake well with ice and strain into a cocktail glass.

According to some sources, this cocktail was created by Phlibert Guichet, the owner of Tujague's bar in New Orleans. It was submitted as an entry to a New York cocktail contest held, amazingly enough, just before Prohibition was repealed.

Grasshopper

Guadalajara

(by Robert Hess, 2001)

- •2 ounces (60ml) tequila
- •1 ounce (30ml) dry vermouth
- •½ ounce (15ml) Bénédictine

Stir with ice and strain into a cocktail glass.

Garnish with lemon twist.

I created this drink while trying to come up with something new that used Bénédictine. You might notice the similarities between this drink and the Black Feather.

Guinness Punch

- •8 ounces (240ml) Guinness stout
- •5 ounces (150ml) sweetened condensed milk
- •1 raw egg
- •Sprinkle of cinnamon
- •Sprinkle of nutmeg

Mix all ingredients in a blender or with a whisk.

Pour into a tall glass.

Garnish with an additional sprinkle of cinnamon and nutmeg.

This is apparently a popular drink in Jamaica. My introduction to it came while watching the BBC comedy Chef!

and after a little research was able to track down the recipe.

Harrington

(by Paul Harrington)

- •1½ ounce (45ml) vodka
- •¼ ounce (7ml) Cointreau
- •⅛ ounce (4ml) green Chartreuse

Stir with ice and strain into a cocktail glass.

Twist an orange zest over the drink and then float zest in drink.

Paul simply called this drink "The Drink with No Name," which I felt was a cop out. It's a great drink, and so I've boldly named it after him.

1998

Harvard

- 1½ ounce (45ml) brandy
- ¾ ounce (22ml) sweet vermouth
- ¼ ounce (7ml) grenadine
- ½ ounce (15ml) lemon juice

Dash of Angostura bitters

Shake with ice and strain into a cocktail glass.

Hemingway Daiquiri

- 1½ ounce (45ml) white rum
- ¼ ounce (7ml) maraschino liqueur
- ½ ounce (15ml) grapefruit juice
- ¾ ounce (22ml) simple syrup
- ¾ ounce (22ml) lime juice

Shake with ice and strain into a chilled cocktail glass.

Sometimes this drink is also referred to as "Papa Doble." It's a classic variation of the Daiquiri and was popular at the El Floridita bar in Havana, Cuba. Hemingway preferred his without the sugar (simple syrup) supposedly because he was being careful about his diabetes.

Highland Cocktail

- 1½ ounce (45ml) Scotch whisky
- 1½ ounce (45ml) sweet vermouth
- 1 dash orange bitters

Stir with ice and strain into a cocktail glass.

Hoskins

(by Chuck Taggart, 2003)

- 2 ounces (60ml) Plymouth gin
- ¾ ounce (22ml) Torani Amer
- ½ ounce (15ml) maraschino liqueur
- ¼ ounce (7ml) Cointreau
- 1 dash orange bitters

Stir with ice and strain into a cocktail glass.

Flame an orange peel over the drink and garnish with the peel.

"This cocktail was created to feature the flavor of Torani Amer, an American version of the French bitter orange apéritif Amer Picon. Picon is more readily available in Europe, and is an acceptable substitute, but the best flavor comes from the Torani Amer."

-Chuck Taggart

Hot Buttered Rum

Batter mix:

- 1 pound (.45kg) brown sugar
- ¼ pound (.11kg) butter
- Pinch of salt
- ¼ teaspoon (1ml) nutmeg
- ¼ teaspoon (1ml) cloves
- ½ teaspoon (2.5ml) cinnamon

Combine all ingredients and stir together until well blended and creamy.

In a pre-heated coffee mug, drop in 1 heaping teaspoon (5+ml) of the above batter.

Add 2 ounces (60ml) of rum.

Top with hot water.

Stir well.

Garnish with grated nutmeg or dash of cinnamon.

Hot Toddy

- 1½ ounce (45ml) brandy
- ¼ ounce (7ml) lemon juice
- 1 sugar cube (1 teaspoon/5ml), rubbed against the rind of a lemon to infuse it with oils
- 4 ounces (120ml) hot water

Pour into a pre-warmed coffee mug

Stir with a cinnamon stick to dissolve the sugar.

Garnish with a half-slice of lemon.

Income Tax

- 1¼ ounce (37ml) gin
- ¾ ounce (22ml) orange juice
- ¼ ounce (7ml) dry vermouth
- ¼ ounce (7ml) sweet vermouth
- 1 dash Angostura bitters

Shake with ice and strain into a cocktail glass.

1950s promotional drink pamphlet, depicting a Hot Buttered Rum and a Hot Toddy

The Interesting Cocktail

(by Gary Regan)

- 2 ounces (60ml) silver tequila
- ¾ ounce (22ml) Aperol
- ¼ ounce (7ml) dark crème de cacao
- ¼ ounce (7ml) lemon juice
- 4 grapefruit twists

Add everything to an ice-filled mixing glass.

Twist three of the grapefruit peels over the glass, and drop them in.

Shake and then strain into a flute glass.

Garnish with the remaining grapefruit twist.

Gary recommends using a high quality silver tequila in this drink.

Irish Coffee

- 1 teaspoon (5ml) sugar
- 4 ounces (120ml) hot coffee
- 2 ounces (60ml) Irish whiskey
- Dapple of heavy cream

Pre-heat coffee glass with hot water, then empty.

In a pre-heated glass coffee mug or Irish Coffee glass, add the sugar and coffee.

Stir to dissolve.

Then add the whiskey, and add a float of lightly whipped cream on top.

Part of the trick to this drink is whipping the cream until it is just solid enough not to sink through the coffee, but not stiff either. Never use the whipping cream in a pressurized can.

Jack Rose

- 2½ ounces (75ml) applejack
- ¾ ounce (22ml) lemon juice
- ½ ounce (15ml) grenadine

Shake with ice and strain into a cocktail glass.

Garnish with a lemon twist.

This is a lovely and subtle sour-style cocktail. The grenadine you use will make all the difference here. Best to find one made with real pomegranate juice.

Irish Coffee

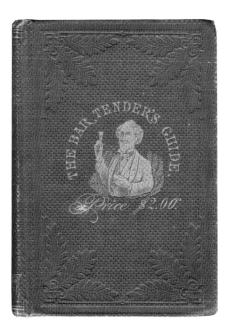

1862, by Jerry Thomas

Japanese

- •2 ounces (60ml) brandy
- •½ ounce (15ml) orgeat (almond syrup)
- •2 dashes Angostura bitters

Stir with ice and strain into a cocktail glass.

Garnish with a lemon twist.

This cocktail appeared in Jerry Thomas's 1862 *Bartender's Guide* but is rarely seen in modern guides. Give it a try, and I expect you'll agree with me that it deserves to be re-discovered.

Jasmine

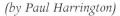

(by Paul Harrington)

- •1½ ounce (45ml) gin
- •¼ ounce (7ml) Cointreau
- •¼ ounce (7ml) Campari
- •¾ ounce (22ml) lemon juice

Shake with ice an strain into a cocktail glass.

Garnish with a lemon twist.

This is Paul Harrington's original recipe. I've tinkered with it a bit to accentuate the flavors. My variation is:

- •1½ ounces (45ml) gin
- •1 ounce (30ml) Cointreau
- •¾ ounce (22ml) Campari
- •½ ounce (15 ml) lemon juice.

I was originally only going to list my version here, but decided to respect Paul's original recipe by listing it first, then providing my interpretation. This illustrates how recipes can be different from one bartender to another.

Joli Rajah

(by Gwydion Stone)

- •2½ ounces (75ml) rum
- •½ ounce (15ml) lemon juice
- •½ ounce (15ml) grenadine
- •½ ounce (15ml) absinthe

Shake with ice and strain into a cocktail glass.

Journalist

- 1½ ounce (45ml) gin
- ¼ ounce (7ml) dry vermouth
- ¼ ounce (7ml) sweet vermouth
- 2 dashes triple sec
- 2 dashes lemon juice
- 1 dash Angostura bitters

Shake with ice and strain into a cocktail glass.

This drink also goes by the name Periodista, which is Spanish for "journalist."

Kamikaze

- 1½ ounce (45ml) vodka
- 1 ounce (30ml) triple sec
- 1 ounce (30ml) lime juice

Shake with ice and strain into a cocktail glass.

Garnish with a lime twist.

This was a very popular drink during the 1980s. Today, many people use lemon juice instead of lime and incorrectly refer to the drink as a Lemon Drop.

Jupiter

- 2 ounces (60ml) gin
- 1 ounce (30ml) dry vermouth
- 1 teaspoon (5ml) orange juice
- 1 teaspoon (5ml) Parfait Amour (orange liqueur)

Shake with ice, and strain into a cocktail glass.

Be extremely careful measuring the Parfait Amour. Too much will ruin the drink. Parfait Amour may be hard to find; Marie Brizard is the most common brand.

Kangaroo

- 1½ ounce (45ml) vodka
- ½ ounce (15ml) dry vermouth

Stir with ice and strain into a cocktail glass.

Garnish with a lemon twist.

This is the proper name for what is sometimes referred to as a Vodka Martini.

Kir

- •5 ounces (150ml) dry white wine (Chardonnay)
- •¼ ounce (7ml) crème de cassis

Pour wine into a wine glass and then add the crème de cassis.

Named after Canon Felix Kir, a former mayor of Dijon, France, who was well known for promoting local products and serving blanc-cassis (the original name for this drink) to visiting dignitaries.

Kir Royale

- •5 ounces (150ml) champagne
- •¼ ounce (7ml) crème de cassis

Fill flute with champagne and add the crème de cassis.

Garnish with a lemon twist.

La Louisiane

- •¾ ounce (22ml) rye whiskey
- •¾ ounce (22ml) sweet vermouth
- •¾ ounce (22ml) Bénédictine
- •3 dashes pastis
- •3 dashes Peychaud's bitters

Stir with ice and strain into a cocktail glass.

Garnish with a cherry.

Introduced as Cocktail a la Louisiane by Stanley Clisby Arthur in *Famous New Orleans Drinks and How to Mix 'Em* (1937). This was the house specialty cocktail of the Restaurant de la Louisiane in New Orleans and is a simply wonderful drink.

Kir Royale

Last Word

- ½ ounce (15ml) gin
- ½ ounce (15ml) maraschino liqueur
- ½ ounce (15ml) green Chartreuse
- ½ ounce (15ml) lime juice

Shake with ice and strain into a cocktail glass.

Long-forgotten, this has recently come back into vogue at better bars across the country.

1951

Leap Year

- 2 ounces (60ml) gin
- ½ ounce (15ml) sweet vermouth
- ½ ounce (15ml) Grand Marnier

Dash of lemon juice

Shake with ice and strain into a cocktail glass.

Lemon Drop

- 1½ ounce (45ml) citrus vodka
- ¾ ounce (22ml) lemon juice
- 1 teaspoon (5ml) sugar

Shake with ice and strain into a sugar-rimmed cocktail glass.

Garnish with a lemon wheel.

This drink is designed to taste like Lemon Drop candies, which are just sugar and lemon flavoring. Many bartenders use triple sec instead of the sugar, and while this results in a great cocktail, it would be more appropriately called a Lemon Kamikaze instead of a Lemon Drop.

Liberal

- 1½ ounce (45ml) rye whiskey
- ½ ounce (15ml) sweet vermouth
- ¼ ounce (7ml) Amer Picon
- 1 dash orange bitters

Stir with ice and strain into a cocktail glass.

Garnish with an orange twist.

If you like Manhattans, then track down some Amer Picon for this drink.

Lucien Gaudin

- 1 ounce (30ml) gin
- ½ ounce (15ml) Cointreau
- ½ ounce (15ml) Campari
- ½ ounce (15ml) dry vermouth

Stir with ice and strain into a cocktail glass.

Garnish with a lemon twist.

This drink is named after Lucien Gaudin, the famous French fencer, who won the gold medal in both the foil and the épée at the 1928 Olympics. Most likely this drink was created around that time to honor his achievements.

Mahogany

(by Robert Hess, 2003)

- 1½ ounce (45ml) dry vermouth
- ¾ ounce (22ml) Jägermeister
- ¾ ounce (22ml) Bénédictine

Stir with ice and strain into a cocktail glass.

Extra Credit: Before adding the drink to the glass, use an atomizer to spray the glass with a mild cinnamon tincture. To make your cinnamon tincture, soak four sticks of cinnamon in 1 cup (250ml) of vodka for about two weeks.

I created this drink after being challenged by a friend to come up with a classically styled cocktail which used Jägermeister. The process taught me a new appreciation for this German digestif.

Mai Tai

(By Victor "Trader Vic" Bergeron, 1944)

- •1 ounce (30ml) light rum
- •1 ounce (30ml) gold rum
- •½ ounce (15ml) orange curaçao
- •½ ounce (15ml) orgeat (almond syrup)
- •½ ounce (15ml) lime juice
- •½ ounce (15ml) dark rum (optional)

Shake all but the dark rum with ice.

Strain into an ice-filled rocks glass.

Top with the dark rum if you wish, then garnish with a maraschino cherry.

This recipe has often been personalized to the point of having little in common with the original. The above version will let you see how this drink was originally intended to be made.

1950s Trader Vic's cocktail menu

Malmo Aviation

(by Sean Muldoon, for the Merchant Hotel, Belfast Northern Ireland)

- 1⅓ ounce (40ml) dry gin
- ⅓ ounce (10ml) Luxardo maraschino liqueur
- ¾ ounce (22ml) lime juice
- ⅓ ounce (10ml) sugar syrup
- 10 mint leaves

Shake with ice and double-strain into a cocktail glass.

Garnish with a cherry.

"This is a marriage of two classic cocktails, the Aviation and the Mojito. I named it after a regional airline of Sweden for no other reason than I liked the name."   -Sean Muldoon

Manhattan

- 2½ ounces (75ml) American rye or bourbon whiskey
- ¾ ounce (22ml) sweet vermouth
- Dash Angostura bitters

Stir with ice and strain into a cocktail glass.

Garnish with a cherry.

This is a veritable classic, which never goes out of style. Make sure you stir instead of shake, otherwise you'll end up with an unappetizing foam on top.

Margarita

- 1½ ounce (45ml) tequila
- 1 ounce (30ml) Cointreau
- ½ ounce (15ml) lime juice

Shake with ice and strain into a salt-rimmed (optional) Old Fashioned glass (rocks), or a salt-rimmed, ice-filled, margarita glass.

Consistently ranked as the most popular cocktail in America, the Margarita is definitely a crowd pleaser. To make this drink properly, you should never use a sour mix, nor should the drink ever see the inside of a blender.

Margarita

Martinez

- 1 ounce (30ml) gin
- 2 ounces (60ml) sweet vermouth
- 1 dash bitters
- 2 dashes maraschino

Stir with ice and strain into a cocktail glass.

Garnish with a lemon twist.

Many feel that this was the original form of the Martini; however, it's more likely a precursor with the Martini being something between a Martinez and a Manhattan.

Martini

(original, sweet)

- 2¼ ounces (67ml) gin
- ¾ ounce (22ml) sweet vermouth
- Dash orange bitters

Stir with ice and strain into a cocktail glass.

Garnish with a cherry or lemon twist.

This recipe represents how this drink would have been made prior to Prohibition, when the art of the cocktail was at its peak.

Martini

(original, dry)

- 2¼ ounces (67ml) gin
- ¾ ounce (22ml) dry vermouth
- Dash orange bitters

Stir with ice and strain into a cocktail glass.

Garnish with a lemon twist or olive.

Prior to Prohibition, a Martini was made with sweet vermouth. If you wanted one with dry vermouth instead, you'd ask for a dry Martini.

Martini

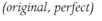

(original, perfect)

- 2¼ ounces (67ml) gin
- ½ ounce (15ml) sweet vermouth
- ½ ounce (15ml) dry vermouth
- Dash orange bitters

Stir with ice and strain into a cocktail glass.

Garnish with a lemon twist.

Just like a Manhattan, a Martini can be ordered normal, dry or perfect. Perfect simply means that the vermouth added to the drink is split between dry and sweet.

Martinez

Martini

(modern)

- 3 ounces (90ml) gin or vodka

Shake with ice.

Strain into a cocktail glass that has been rinsed with dry vermouth.

Garnish with several olives.

I have a hard time calling this a cocktail, much less a Martini, since it's basically just a glass of cold gin or vodka. The three previous Martini recipes are truer Martinis.

Metropole

- 1½ ounce (45ml) brandy
- 1½ ounce (45ml) dry vermouth
- 2 dashes orange bitters
- 1 dash Peychaud's bitters

Stir with ice and strain into a cocktail glass.

Garnish with a cherry.

Milk Punch

- 2 ounces (60ml) bourbon whiskey
- 4 ounces (120ml) milk
- ½ teaspoon (2ml) dark rum
- 1 tablespoon (15ml) simple syrup
- Nutmeg

Shake with ice.

Strain into a chilled 10-ounce (300ml) highball glass with a couple of ice cubes.

Dust with nutmeg.

Mimosa

- 2 ounces (60ml) orange juice
- 4 ounces (120ml) sparkling wine

Pour orange juice into a champagne flute or wine glass and then add the sparkling wine.

This is a favorite brunch drink. Also check out the Buck's Fizz.

Mint Julep

- 3 ounces (90ml) bourbon whiskey
- 4 to 6 sprigs of mint
- 1 ounce (30ml) simple syrup

Muddle the mint and simple syrup in the bottom of a rocks glass or, better yet, a silver mint julep cup.

Add the bourbon and stir to mix.

Fill with finely crushed ice and stir with a swizzle stick until ice begins to form on the outside of the cup.

Top with more crushed ice.

Garnish with a mint sprig and a sprinkle of powdered sugar.

Serve with straws.

It has become common to construct the Mint Julep with what might otherwise be referred to as a frappé process. Of course, there are a variety of other methods associated with this drink. Give this one a try, and if you like it, do a little research to find some of the various other methods and see which one you like the best.

Mix '06

(by Robert Hess, 2006)

- 1 ounce (30ml) gin
- ½ ounce (15ml) Bénédictine
- ¼ ounce (7ml) Campari
- 1 dash Peychaud's bitters
- Top with ginger ale

Shake everything with ice except the ginger ale.

Strain into an ice-filled Collins glass.

Top with ginger ale.

Garnish with a lime twist.

I created this cocktail for a technical conference in Las Vegas called... well... Mix '06. My goal was to create an approachable cocktail using offbeat ingredients.

Mint Julep

Mojito

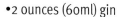

- 2 ounces (60ml) light rum
- 1 ounce (30ml) lime juice
- 2 teaspoons (10ml) sugar
- 4 to 6 sprigs of mint
- Club soda

Place the sugar, mint and a splash of club soda into a highball glass.

Using a muddler, lightly press the mint to extract the oils and dissolve the sugar.

Add the lime juice and rum.

Stir to combine.

Fill the glass with ice and stir to chill.

Top with club soda and garnish with a mint sprig and wedge of lime.

Mojito

Monkey Gland

- 2 ounces (60ml) gin
- 1 ounce (30ml) orange juice
- ¼ ounce (7ml) grenadine
- 1 dash absinthe or pastis

Shake with ice and strain into a cocktail glass.

Garnish with an orange twist.

Monte Carlo

- 2¼ ounces (67ml) rye whiskey
- ¾ ounce (22ml) Bénédictine
- 1 dash Angostura bitters

Stir with ice and strain into a cocktail glass.

Morning Cocktail

- 1½ ounce (45ml) brandy
- 1½ ounce (45ml) dry vermouth
- 2 dashes orange curaçao
- 2 dashes maraschino liqueur
- 2 dashes orange bitters
- 2 dashes absinthe or pastis

Stir with ice and strain into a cocktail glass.

Garnish with a cherry and lemon twist.

Moscow Mule

Moscow Mule

- •2 ounces (60ml) vodka
- •3 ounces (90ml) ginger beer
- •1 ounce (30ml) lime juice

Build in an ice-filled highball glass or copper mug.

Garnish with a lime wedge.

Dating from around 1946, this was perhaps the first drink created in America that specifically used vodka.

Mother-In-Law

- •2 ounces (60ml) bourbon
- •1 teaspoon (5ml) Cointreau
- •1 teaspoon (5ml) maraschino liqueur
- •1 teaspoon (5ml) simple syrup
- •2 dashes Peychaud's bitters
- •2 dashes Angostura bitters
- •2 dashes Amer Picon

Stir with ice and strain into a cocktail glass.

Garnish with a cherry.

Morris Cocktail

(by Jamie Boudreau, for Vessel in Seattle, Washington)

- •1½ ounce (45ml) bourbon whiskey
- •1 ounce (30ml) Lillet Blanc
- •½ ounce (15ml) sweet vermouth
- •1 dash orange bitters
- •1 dash of simple syrup

Stir with ice and strain into a cocktail glass.

Garnish with an orange twist.

Jamie recommends using Woodford Reserve bourbon whiskey, Fee Brothers orange bitters and Amaro Nonino for the sweet vermouth.

Naciónal

(by Francesco Lafranconi)

- 1½ ounce (45ml) rum
- 2 wedges of lime
- 2 dashes Angostura bitters
- Fresh mint
- 4 ounces (120ml) cola
- ½ ounce (15ml) amaretto

Muddle lime, mint and bitters in a highball glass.

Add ice and rum.

Fill with cola and then add a float of amaretto.

Garnish with a sprig of mint.

Francesco recommends using 10 Cane rum and Disaronno amaretto.

"This drink was developed on a hot summer day in Las Vegas. The rhum agricole flavor of 10 Cane rum combined with bitters, mint and cola is just a great match and the touch of Disaronno brings a hint of nuttiness."
-Francesco Lafranconi

Negroni

- 1 ounce (30ml) gin
- 1 ounce (30ml) sweet vermouth
- 1 ounce (30ml) Campari

Stir with ice and strain into a cocktail glass. (It's not uncommon to strain the drink into an ice-filled rocks glass.)

Garnish with a lemon twist or an orange slice.

Negroni

Nicky Finn

- 1 ounce (30ml) brandy
- 1 ounce (30ml) Cointreau
- 1 ounce (30ml) lemon juice
- Dash absinthe or pastis

Shake with ice and strain into a cocktail glass.

Garnish with cherry or a lemon twist.

Nightwatch

(by Robert Hess, 2006)

- 1 ounce (30ml) gin
- 1 ounce (30ml) coffee liqueur
- ¼ ounce (7ml) absinthe or pastis

Shake with ice and strain into a cocktail glass.

This drink was designed as part of the Spirited Dinners of the annual *Tales of the Cocktail* event at Antoine's Restaurant in New Orleans. It's meant to accompany Baked Alaska or a similar style dessert.

Obituary Cocktail

- 2 ounces (60ml) gin
- ¼ ounce (7ml) dry vermouth
- ¼ ounce (7ml) absinthe or absinthe substitute

Stir with ice and strain into a cocktail glass.

This drink is believed to have been created at Lafitte's Blacksmith Shop in New Orleans as a local variation of the dry Martini.

Old Fashioned

- 1 sugar cube (1 teaspoon/ 5ml)
- 1 teaspoon (5ml) water
- 2 dashes Angostura bitters
- 2 ounces (60ml) American rye or bourbon whiskey

Muddle sugar, water and bitters together until the sugar is mostly dissolved.

Fill glass with ice, and then add the whiskey and stir briefly to chill.

Garnish with a twist of orange peel and a cherry.

Serve with straws.

A truly classic cocktail, the Old Fashioned has unfortunately fallen on hard times lately, possibly because of all the horrendous ways it's being made. Give the above recipe a try and you'll wonder that it isn't ordered more often.

Old Fashioned

Old Hickory

- 1 ounce (30ml) dry vermouth
- 1 ounce (30ml) sweet vermouth
- 1 dash orange bitters
- 2 dashes Peychaud's bitters

Stir with ice and strain into a cocktail glass.

Garnish with a lemon twist.

Andrew Jackson was said to be particularly fond of this drink, so fond that his troops nicknamed him "Old Hickory."

Old Pal

- 1½ ounce (45ml) rye or bourbon whiskey
- ¾ ounce (22ml) dry vermouth
- ¾ ounce (22ml) Campari

Stir with ice and strain into a cocktail glass.

Garnish with a lemon twist.

Opera

- 2 ounces (60ml) gin
- ½ ounce (15ml) Dubonnet rouge
- ¼ ounce (7ml) maraschino liqueur
- 1 dash orange bitters

Stir with ice and strain into a cocktail glass.

Garnish with a lemon twist.

Palm Beach Special

- 2 ounces (60ml) gin
- ½ ounce (15ml) sweet vermouth
- ½ ounce (15ml) grapefruit juice

Shake with ice and strain into a cocktail glass.

Parisian

- 1½ ounce (45ml) gin
- 1½ ounce (45ml) dry vermouth
- ½ ounce (15ml) crème de cassis

Stir with ice and strain into a cocktail glass.

Garnish with a lemon twist.

Park Avenue

- 2 ounces (60ml) gin
- 1 ounce (30ml) pineapple juice
- ½ ounce (15ml) sweet vermouth
- Dash orange curaçao

Shake with ice.

Strain into a cocktail glass.

Parkside Fizz

(by Jim Meehan, for PDT in New York)

- 2 ounces (60ml) citrus vodka
- ¾ ounce (22ml) lemon juice
- ½ ounce (30ml) orgeat (almond syrup)
- 6-8 mint leaves
- 1 ounce (30ml) club soda

Muddle the mint and orgeat in a mixing glass.

Add all but the club soda and shake with ice.

Strain into an ice-filled rocks glass.

Top with club soda and garnish with a mint sprig.

Jim recommends using Hangar One Buddha's Hand for the vodka in this drink.

Pegu

- 2 ounces (60ml) gin
- 1 ounce (30ml) orange curaçao
- 1 teaspoon (5 ml) lime juice
- 1 dash Angostura bitters
- 1 dash orange bitters

Shake with ice and strain into a cocktail glass.

Garnish with a lime wedge.

This was the signature drink at the Pegu Club, a British club in Rangoon. An early recipe appeared in Harry McElhone's 1927 *Barflies and Cocktails*.

Pegu

Pepper Delirious

(by Ryan Magarian)

- 2 thin yellow bell pepper rings
- ⅔ cup (40g) loosely packed mint
- 2 ounces (60ml) gin
- ¾ ounce (22ml) lemon juice
- ¾ ounce (22ml) simple syrup

Muddle everything together in a mixing glass without ice.

Shake with ice and strain into a cocktail glass.

Garnish with a mint sprig and thin ring of yellow pepper.

Ryan recommends using Aviation gin to make this drink.

"I created this for the opening of the Phillipe Starck designed S-Bar. This simple variation on a classic Gimlet was created to be 'deliciously obtuse' mimicking the wild interior of the bar itself."   -Ryan Magarian

Petit Zinc

(by Paul Harrington)

- 1 ounce (30ml) vodka
- ½ ounce (15ml) Cointreau
- ½ ounce (15ml) sweet vermouth
- ½ ounce (15ml) orange juice (use fresh-squeezed Seville oranges; if not available, add ¼ ounce (7ml) lemon juice to recipe).

Shake with ice and strain into a cocktail glass.

Garnish with a wedge of orange.

Paul came up with this recipe trying to recreate a drink one of his customers remembers having on a trip to Paris.

Picon Cremaillere

- 1½ ounce (45ml) gin
- ¾ ounce (22ml) Amer Picon
- ¾ ounce (22ml) Dubonnet rouge
- 1 dash orange bitters

Stir with ice and strain into a cocktail glass.

Pepper Delirious

Pimm's Cup

Picon Punch

- 2 ounces (60ml) Amer Picon
- ½ ounce (15ml) lemon juice
- ½ ounce (15ml) grenadine
- 4 ounces (120ml) club soda

Shake the Amer Picon, lemon juice and grenadine with ice.

Strain into an ice-filled highball glass.

Top with club soda.

Garnish with seasonal fruits.

Pimm's Cup

- 2 ounces (60ml) Pimm's No. 1
- 3 ounces (90ml) ginger ale
- Cucumber

Pour Pimm's into a highball glass.

Fill with ice and top with ginger ale or lemon/lime soda.

Garnish with a wedge of lemon and a slice of cucumber.

This drink can also be properly prepared by garnishing it with a variety of fruits and berries in season.

Piña Colada

- 2 ounces (60ml) white rum
- 1 ounce (30ml) coconut cream
- 1 ounce (30ml) heavy cream
- 6 ounces (180ml) pineapple juice
- 4 ounces (120ml) crushed ice

Blend all ingredients with crushed ice until it just reaches a smooth consistency.

Pour into a wine goblet and garnish with pineapple spear and cherry.

The Piña Colada was introduced at the Caribe Hilton's Beachcomber Bar on August 15, 1954.

Piña Colada

Piña Partida

(by Junior Merino)

- •2 chunks pineapple
- •2 slices cucumber
- •3 lemon wedges
- •⅓ ounce (10ml) simple syrup
- •1½ ounce (45ml) silver tequila
- •½ ounce (15ml) lemon/lime soda

Muddle the pineapple, cucumber, lemon and simple syrup.

Add the tequila and shake with ice.

Strain into an ice-filled highball glass and top with lemon/lime soda.

Garnish with a slice of cucumber.

In keeping with the name of the drink, Junior recommends using Partida Blanco for the tequila as well as agave syrup instead of simple syrup.

Pink Gin

- •1½ ounce (45ml) gin
- •3 or 4 dashes Angostura bitters

Stir with ice and strain into a cocktail glass.

Pink Gin and Tonic

(by Dale DeGroff, for Plymouth Gin)

- •1½ ounce (45ml) Plymouth Gin
- •2 dashes Peychaud's bitters
- •2 sage leaves
- •4 ounces (120ml) tonic water

Lightly muddle sage leaves in the bottom of a highball glass.

Fill the glass with ice.

Add the gin, bitters and tonic water.

Stir briefly.

Dale recommends using Plymouth for the gin and a high quality tonic water (Schweppes or Fever Tree).

Pink Lady

- •1½ ounce (45ml) gin
- •½ ounce (15ml) applejack
- •¾ ounce (22ml) lemon juice
- •¼ ounce (7ml) grenadine
- •1 egg white

Shake with ice and strain into a wine glass.

This is essentially the same as the Clover Club but with the addition of applejack. Ted "Dr. Cocktail" Haigh prefers to call this drink the "Secret Cocktail" so that grown men won't be embarrassed to order it.

Pisco Sour

- 2¼ ounce (67ml) pisco
- ¾ ounce (22ml) lime juice
- ¾ ounce (22ml) simple syrup
- 1 whole egg white
- Several dashes Angostura bitters.

Shake hard with ice to build up a good foam.

Strain into a flute or sour glass.

Use the bitters as an aromatic garnish to top the finished drink.

Pisco Sour

Planters Punch

- 1 ounce (30ml) dark rum
- 1 ounce (30ml) light rum
- ½ ounce (15ml) orange curaçao
- 2 ounces (60ml) orange juice
- 2 ounces (60ml) pineapple juice
- ½ ounce (15ml) simple syrup
- ¼ ounce (7ml) lime juice
- 1 dash grenadine
- 1 dash Angostura bitters

Shake all ingredients well with ice and strain into an iced Collins glass.

Top with a small amount of club soda.

Garnish with an orange slice and cherry.

Like all punch drinks, topping with club soda is optional.

If you try to find the definitive recipe for a Planters Punch, you might drive yourself to drink. This is just one of many variations.

Poet's Dream

- ¾ ounce (22ml) gin
- ¾ ounce (22ml) dry vermouth
- ¾ ounce (22ml) Bénédictine

Stir with ice and strain into a cocktail glass.

Garnish with a lemon twist.

Port Wine Cocktail

- 2 ounces (60ml) ruby port
- Dash brandy

Stir with ice and strain into a cocktail glass.

Garnish with a lemon twist.

Precious Thyme

(by Francesco Lafranconi)

- 1 ounce (30ml) Campari
- 1 ounce (30ml) limoncello
- 1 ounce (30ml) sweet vermouth
- 2 ounces (60ml) club soda
- 1 sprig of fresh thyme

Pour ingredients into an ice-filled highball glass and stir.

Garnish with the thyme, an orange slice and a lemon twist.

Francesco recommends using Cinzano sweet vermouth in this drink.

"As a fan of bitters and apéritifs, I wanted to make this drink accessible to guests who aren't overly fond of the aromatic-bitter component. I added limoncello and a sprig of thyme to lace all the ingredients together. It's definitively a very friendly approach with a full Italian character."

-Francesco Lafranconi

Pusser's Painkiller

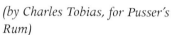

(by Charles Tobias, for Pusser's Rum)

- 2 ounces (60ml) Pusser's rum
- 4 ounces (120ml) unsweetened pineapple juice
- 1 ounce (30ml) orange juice
- 1 ounce (30ml) coconut cream

Shake with ice and strain into an ice-filled Collins glass or Tiki mug.

Garnish with ground nutmeg, cinnamon, pineapple stick and orange wheel.

1930

Ramos Gin Fizz

- 2 ounces (60ml) gin
- 1 ounce (30ml) cream
- 1 whole egg white
- ½ ounce (15ml) lemon juice
- ½ ounce (15ml) lime juice
- 1¼ ounce (37ml) simple syrup
- 2 dashes orange flower water
- 1 ounce (30ml) club soda

Minus the club soda and without ice, shake all ingredients very hard to quicken the emulsification.

Add ice and shake some more (at least a minute), resulting in a fairly foamy consistency. Strain into a Collins glass with a few cubes of ice and top with the club soda.

This is a classic New Orleans cocktail invented in the 1880s by Henry C. Ramos at his bar in Meyer's Restaurant. The original recipe required 12 minutes of shaking to achieve the proper creamy consistency. You could try that to see if you like the results better.

Red Snapper

- 2 ounces (60ml) gin
- 4 ounces (120ml) tomato juice
- ½ ounce (15ml) lemon juice
- Pinch of salt and pepper
- 2 to 3 dashes Worcestershire sauce
- 2 to 3 drops Tabasco sauce

Stir all ingredients with ice in a highball glass.

Garnish with a celery stalk and a lemon wedge.

This is essentially just a Bloody Mary made with gin instead of vodka. You can practice the same creative enhancements to this drink as you might a Bloody Mary.

The Reluctant Tabby Cat

(by Gary Regan)

- 1¼ ounces (37ml) Dubonnet rouge
- ½ ounce (15ml) limoncello
- ¼ ounce (7ml) Scotch whisky

Shake with ice and strain into a wine goblet.

Garnish with a lemon twist.

Gary recommends using Pallini Limoncello and Laphroaig Single Malt Scotch for this drink.

Remsen Cooler

- 2 ounces (60ml) Scotch whisky
- 4 ounces (120ml) club soda

Garnish a Collins glass with a long and wide spiral of lemon peel (try to peel the whole lemon in one long spiral about ¾ inch/19mm wide), with the spiral hanging partially out of the glass.

Add a few ice cubes and then the scotch.

Top with club soda.

Said to be named after the no-longer available Remsen Scotch and considered by some to be the original cooler.

Renaissance

(by Robert Hess, 2002)

- 2 ounces (60ml) brandy
- 1 ounce (30ml) sweet vermouth
- ¼ ounce (7ml) limoncello
- 2 dashes peach bitters

Stir with ice and train into a cocktail glass.

Garnish with a lemon twist.

I created this drink to focus on an Italian angle with the sweet vermouth and limoncello as well as to experiment with peach bitters.

Retreat

(by David Nepove, 1st place in StarChef.com cocktail competition)

- 1 ounce (30ml) lemon juice
- ½ ounce (15ml) simple syrup
- 5 basil leaves
- 1½ ounce (45ml) citrus vodka
- ½ ounce (15ml) Pernod
- 2 ounces (60ml) club soda

Muddle the basil in lemon juice and simple syrup.

Add vodka and the Pernod and shake with ice.

Double strain into an ice-filled Collins glass and top with club soda.

Garnish with a sprig of basil and a lemon twist.

David uses Absolut Citron for this drink.

Robert Burns

- 2¼ ounce (67ml) Scotch whisky
- ¾ ounce (22ml) sweet vermouth
- 1 dash orange bitters
- 1 dash absinthe or pastis

Stir with ice and strain into a cocktail glass.

Rob Roy

- 2¼ ounce (67ml) Scotch whisky
- ¾ ounce (22ml) sweet vermouth
- 1 dash orange bitters

Stir with ice and strain into a cocktail glass.

Garnish with lemon twist.

This is essentially a Manhattan made with Scotch whisky instead of American. Like a Manhattan, it can be made with Angostura bitters instead of orange.

Rob Roy

Rose

- 2 ounces (60ml) dry vermouth
- 1 ounce (30ml) kirschwasser
- 1 teaspoon (5ml) raspberry or red currant syrup

Stir with ice and strain into a cocktail glass.

Garnish with a cherry.

Invented at the Chatham Bar in Paris by Johnny Mitta around 1922.

Rosita

- 1½ ounce (45ml) silver tequila
- ½ ounce (15ml) sweet vermouth
- ½ ounce (15ml) dry vermouth
- ½ ounce (15ml) Campari
- 1 dash Angostura bitters

Stir with ice and strain into an ice-filled rocks glass.

Garnish with lemon twist.

This is an excellent cocktail to celebrate, rather than mask, the flavor of tequila. Unfortunately, it is rarely seen in cocktail manuals.

Rubicon

(by Jamie Boudreau, for Vessel in Seattle)

- ½ ounce (15ml) green Chartreuse
- 1 rosemary sprig
- 2 ounces (60ml) gin
- ½ ounce (15ml) maraschino liqueur
- ½ ounce (15ml) lemon juice

Curl the rosemary sprig into the bottom of a rocks glass.

Add the Chartreuse.

Light the Chartreuse and allow to burn while you mix the drink.

Shake the gin, maraschino liqueur and lemon juice with ice.

Strain into the glass to extinguish the flame.

Top with crushed ice.

"For a little added flare, I keep some Chartreuse in a fancy misting bottle, and use this as a torch to light the chartreuse by holding a match in front of the nozzle."   - Jamie Boudreau

Rusty Nail

- 1½ ounce (45ml) Scotch whisky
- ½ ounce (15ml) Drambuie

Stir with ice and strain into an ice-filled rocks glass.

Saratoga

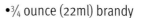

- ¾ ounce (22ml) brandy
- ¾ ounce (22ml) rye whiskey
- ¾ ounce (22ml) sweet vermouth
- 2 dashes Angostura bitters

Stir with ice and strain into a cocktail glass.

Garnish with a slice of lemon.

This venerable but forgotten cocktail dates from the 1800s and is great for anyone who loves a Manhattan or similar drink.

Satan's Whiskers

- ¾ ounce (22ml) gin
- ¾ ounce (22ml) dry vermouth
- ¾ ounce (22ml) sweet vermouth
- ½ ounce (15ml) orange juice
- ½ ounce (15ml) Grand Marnier
- 1 dash orange bitters

Shake with ice and strain into a cocktail glass.

You can use orange curaçao instead of Grand Marnier in which case this would be *curled*.

Rubicon

Sazerac

Sazerac

- •1 sugar cube (1 teaspoon/5ml)
- •1 teaspoon (5ml) water
- •2 dashes Peychaud's bitters
- •3 ounces (90ml) rye whiskey
- •1 teaspoon (5ml) absinthe or absinthe substitute

Prepare a small rocks glass by coating it with absinthe.

Put the sugar, water and bitters into a mixing glass and muddle to dissolve the sugar and form a syrup.

Add the rye to the mixing glass and fill the glass with ice and stir.

Strain into the rocks glass.

Garnish with a lemon twist.

Variation: You can use simple syrup instead of the sugar cube and water to avoid undissolved sugar remaining in the drink.

Some stories tie the Sazerac to the origin of the cocktail. Unfortunately this drink is reliant on Peychaud's bitters which didn't come onto the scene until at least 30 years after the cocktail was well established.

Scofflaw

- •1 ounce (30ml) Canadian whisky
- •1 ounce (30ml) dry vermouth
- •¼ ounce (7ml) lemon juice
- •Dash of grenadine
- •Dash of orange bitters

Stir with ice and strain into a cocktail glass.

Garnish with a lemon wedge.

In the middle of Prohibition, a contest was held to find a word to describe someone who flouted the laws against alcohol consumption. The winning entry was scofflaw. Of course, it didn't take long for a drink to be christened by that name. It used Canadian whisky, since that was the spirit which replaced American whiskey during Prohibition.

Scottish Guard

- •1½ ounce (45ml) bourbon whiskey
- •½ ounce (15ml) lemon juice
- •½ ounce (15ml) orange juice
- •1 teaspoon (5ml) grenadine

Shake with ice and strain into a cocktail glass.

Seattle Manhattan

(by Ryan Magarian)

- 2 ounces (60ml) bourbon whiskey
- ½ ounce (15ml) sweet vermouth
- ½ ounce (15ml) coffee liqueur

Stir with ice and strain into a cocktail glass.

Garnish with three coffee beans.

Ryan suggests using Knob Creek bourbon whiskey and Starbucks coffee liqueur.

"I created this for the launch of Starbucks Coffee Liqueur."

-Ryan Magarian

Seattle Manhattan

Sidecar

- 2 ounces (60ml) brandy (cognac)
- 1 ounce (30ml) Cointreau
- ½ ounce (15ml) lemon juice

Shake with ice and strain into cocktail glass.

Sugar, while not part of the original recipe, is commonly used to rim the glass. I think this just leaves you with sticky fingers.

Silk Stockings

- 1 ounce (30ml) tequila
- ¾ ounce (22ml) white crème de cacao
- ¾ ounce (22ml) cream
- Dash of grenadine

Shake hard with ice to froth the cream a little.

Strain into a cocktail glass.

Garnish with a sprinkle of nutmeg.

Without the grenadine this would be a Frostbite.

Singapore Sling

- 1½ ounce (45ml) gin
- ½ ounce (15ml) Cherry Heering Liqueur
- ¼ ounce (7ml) Cointreau
- ¼ ounce (7ml) Bénédictine
- 4 ounces (120ml) pineapple juice
- ½ ounce (15ml) lime juice
- ⅓ ounce (10ml) grenadine
- Dash bitters

Shake with ice and strain into an ice-filled Collins glass.

Garnish with cherry and slice of pineapple.

The Singapore Sling was created by Mr. Ngiam Tong Boon for the Raffles Hotel in Singapore around 1915. It is believed that the original recipe was actually forgotten and had to be recreated from scribbled notes on the back of a napkin. The recipe listed here is what has been the official recipe since around 1930.

Southside

- 1½ ounce (45ml) gin
- ¾ ounce (22ml) lemon juice
- ½ ounce (15ml) simple syrup

Shake with ice and strain into a cocktail glass.

Garnish with mint sprigs.

Thought to have originated in Prohibition Chicago, this drink was possibly created as a way for Southside mobsters to drink their rather cheap gin. Northside gangsters preferred to mix their gin with ginger ale for the same purpose.

Spanish Bay

(by Chris Hannah, for Arnaud's French 75 bar in New Orleans)

- 1 ounce (30ml) sherry
- 1 ounce (30ml) green Chartreuse
- 1 ounce (30ml) orange juice

Shake with ice and strain into a cocktail glass.

Chris recommends using Dry Sack sherry.

Spanish Rose

(by David Nepove)

- 1½ ounce (45ml) gin
- ¾ ounce (22ml) Licor 43
- ½ ounce (15ml) lemon juice
- ¼ ounce (7ml) cranberry juice
- 1 sprig rosemary

Muddle half of the rosemary sprig in the lemon juice and Licor 43.

Add the gin and shake with ice.

Double strain into an ice-filled Collins glass.

Add the cranberry juice.

Garnish with the other half of rosemary.

David recommends using Tanqueray gin.

Stargazer

(by Robert Hess, 2006)

- 1½ ounce (45ml) rye whiskey
- 1½ ounce (45ml) Lillet Blanc
- 1 dash Angostura bitters

Stir with ice and strain into a cocktail glass.

Garnish with a lemon twist.

This cocktail was created as part of dinner at Antoine's in New Orleans to accompany their grilled trout with crawfish tails/shrimp in a white wine sauce.

Stork Club

- 1½ ounce (45ml) gin
- ½ ounce (15ml) Cointreau
- 1 ounce (30ml) orange juice
- ¼ ounce (7ml) lime juice
- 1 dash Angostura bitters

Shake with ice and strain into a cocktail glass.

Garnish with an orange peel.

The Stork Club was a famous speakeasy in New York. It opened just prior to the end of Prohibition.

1946

Stinger

- •1 ounce (30ml) brandy
- •¼ ounce (7ml) crème de menthe (white)

Stir with ice and strain into a cocktail glass.

Garnish with fresh sprigs of mint, and serve with a glass of ice water.

At Christmastime this can be a festive drink made with green crème de menthe and garnished with a maraschino cherry. This alteration should only be done during the holidays.

Straits Sling

- •2 ounces (60ml) gin
- •½ ounce (15ml) dry cherry brandy
- •½ ounce (15ml) Bénédictine
- •1 ounce (30ml) lemon juice
- •2 dashes of orange bitters
- •2 dashes of Angostura bitters

Shake with ice and strain into an ice-filled Collins glass.

Fill with club soda.

Some feel this might have been the original version of the Singapore Sling.

Strega Daiquiri

- •1 ounce (30ml) light rum
- •1 ounce (30ml) Strega
- •½ ounce (15ml) lemon juice
- •½ ounce (15ml) orange juice
- •½ teaspoon (2.5ml) orgeat (almond syrup)

Shake with ice and strain into a cocktail glass.

Garnish with a cherry.

Strega is an Italian liqueur that is often hard to find, but it has an excellent complex slightly sweet flavor.

Sweet Heat

(by David Nepove, 1st place Gran Centenario Cocktail Competition, 2002)

- •2 ounces (60ml) tequila
- •½ jalapeño (with seeds removed)
- •1 ounce (30ml) lime juice
- •1 ounce (30ml) simple syrup
- •1 ounce (30ml) Licor 43

Muddle the jalapeño in the lime juice and simple syrup.

Add the tequila and shake with ice.

Strain into an ice-filled Collins glass.

Garnish with a lime wheel.

David uses Gran Centinario Añejo for the tequila.

Tailspin

- ¾ ounce (22ml) gin
- ¾ ounce (22ml) sweet vermouth
- ¾ ounce (22ml) green Chartreuse
- 1 dash Campari

Stir with ice and strain into a cocktail glass.

Garnish with lemon twist and cherry.

Many recipes list the Tailspin as being exactly the same at the Bijou. However, I feel that the dash of Campari instead of orange bitters provides an interesting and exciting twist to this drink.

Tango

- ½ ounce (15ml) rum
- ½ ounce (15ml) sweet vermouth
- ½ ounce (15ml) dry vermouth
- ½ ounce (15ml) Bénédictine
- ½ ounce (15ml) orange juice

Shake with ice and strain into a cocktail glass.

Garnish with an orange twist.

Ti Punch

- 1½ ounce (45ml) rum
- ¼ ounce (7ml) simple syrup
- Thin slice of lime peel

Add everything to a small rocks glass with a small piece of ice.

Stir and serve.

Traditionally this would be made with rhum agricole, which is a rum made from sugar instead of molasses.

Tillicum

(by Robert Hess)

- 2¼ ounces (67ml) gin
- ¾ ounce (22ml) dry vermouth
- 2 dashes Peychaud's bitters

Stir with ice and strain into a cocktail glass.

Garnish with a slice of raw smoked salmon skewered flat on a pick.

I created this drink while playing around with Martinis that used different garnishes. The name comes from the traditional way Indians from Tillicum Village would prepare their salmon for cooking around the fire. This is reflected in the salmon garnish.

Tillicum

Tip Top

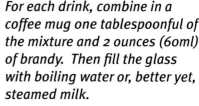

- 2 ounces (60ml) dry vermouth
- ¼ ounce (7ml) Bénédictine
- 2 dashes Angostura bitters

Stir with ice and strain into a cocktail glass.

Garnish with a lemon twist.

Tom and Jerry

Batter mix:

3 eggs, whites and yolks separated
- ½ ounce (15ml) rum
- ½ teaspoon (2.5ml) cinnamon
- Dash cloves
- Dash allspice
- Dash cream of tartar
- Dash vanilla
- ½ cup (115g) sugar

In one bowl, beat the egg whites to a stiff froth.

In another bowl, beat the yolks until they are as thin as water.

Mix yolks and whites together and add the rum and spices.

Thicken with sugar until the mixture attains the consistency of a light batter.

For each drink, combine in a coffee mug one tablespoonful of the mixture and 2 ounces (60ml) of brandy. Then fill the glass with boiling water or, better yet, steamed milk.

Garnish by grating a little nutmeg on top.

As tradition dictates, this drink should only be made after the first snowfall.

Tom Collins

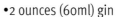

- 2 ounces (60ml) gin
- ¾ ounce (22ml) lemon juice
- 1 teaspoon (5ml) superfine sugar or simple syrup
- 2 ounces (60ml) club soda

Shake with ice and strain into an ice-filled Collins glass.

Top with club soda and garnish with a cherry and orange wheel.

Trident

(by Robert Hess, 2002)

- •1 ounce (30ml) dry sherry
- •1 ounce (30ml) Cynar
- •1 ounce (30ml) aquavit
- •2 dashes peach bitters

Stir with ice and strain into a cocktail glass.

Garnish with a lemon twist.

Clearly based on the Negroni, this drink reflects my penchant for slightly obscure products not normally found in bars. The Zig Zag Cafe in Seattle has had this on their menu for several years, and because of it, the Zig Zag uses more Cynar than all the other bars in Washington State combined.

Trident

Twentieth Century Cocktail

- •1½ ounce (45ml) gin
- •¾ ounce (22ml) Lillet Blanc
- •¾ ounce (22ml) lemon juice
- •½ ounce (15ml) white crème de cacao

Shake with ice and strain into a cocktail glass.

Twenty-first Century Cocktail

(by Jim Meehan, for PDT in New York)

- •1½ ounce (45ml) silver or blanco tequila
- •¾ ounce (22ml) white crème de cacao
- •¾ ounce (22ml) lemon juice
- •¼ ounce (7ml) absinthe or pastis

Prepare a cocktail glass by pouring in the absinthe or pastis, then swirl to coat and dump the liquid.

Shake everything else with ice and strain into the prepared cocktail glass.

Jim recommends using Herradura or Partida tequila and Marie Brizard crème de cacao.

Tyrol

- ½ ounce (15ml) brandy
- ½ ounce (15ml) green Chartreuse
- 1 ounce (30ml) Galliano
- ½ ounce (15ml) cream

Shake with ice and strain into a cocktail glass.

Garnish with nutmeg.

Union Club

(by Jamie Boudreau, for Vessel in Seattle)

- 2 ounces (60ml) bourbon whiskey
- ½ ounce (15ml) maraschino liqueur
- ½ ounce (15ml) Campari
- 1½ ounce (45ml) orange juice

Shake with ice and strain into a cocktail glass.

FLEISCHMANN'S MIXER'S MANUAL

1950s

Union Club

Velvet Harvest

Velvet Harvest

(by Chad Solomon)

- •2 ounces (60ml) pear brandy
- •½ ounce (15ml) falernum
- •½ ounce (15ml) apple schnapps
- •¼ ounce (7ml) maple syrup
- •½ ounce (15ml) lemon juice
- •1 egg white
- •2 dashes Angostura bitters
- •2 dashes clove tincture*

Shake vigorously with ice to emulsify the egg white and then strain into a cocktail glass.

Garnish with 3 additional drops of clove tincture and a pear slice.

*clove tincture- combine 1 ounce (30g) of whole cloves and 8 ounces (240ml) of vodka in a glass container and seal. Let infuse for two weeks, and then strain into a dasher bottle.

Chad recommends using Clear Creek Poire Eau de Vie for the pear brandy and Velvet Falernum.

"I created this cocktail centered around classic autumn flavors--clove, apple and maple syrup. Note: It is very important to thoroughly shake this cocktail. My personal trick is to whip or dry shake drinks with egg white before I add ice to pre-emulsify the egg. This helps to produce a frothy velvety texture."

- Chad Solomon

Vesper

- •3 ounces (90ml) gin
- •1 ounce (30ml) vodka
- •½ ounce (15ml) Lillet Blanc

Stir with ice and strain into a cocktail glass.

Garnish with lemon twist.

Reputedly, Gilberto Preti at London's Duke's Hotel created this drink specifically for Ian Fleming to use in his first James Bond novel *Casino Royale*.

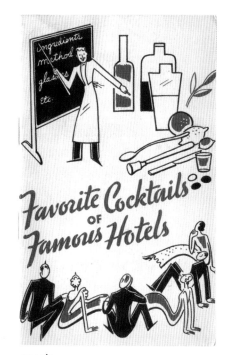

1940's

Vieux Carré

- ¾ ounce (22ml) rye whiskey
- ¾ ounce (22ml) brandy
- ¾ ounce (22ml) sweet vermouth
- ¼ ounce (7ml) Bénédictine
- 1 dash Peychaud's bitters
- 1 dash Angostura bitters

Build over ice in a rocks glass.

Garnish with a lemon twist.

This drink was created in the 1930s at what is now the Carousel Bar in the Hotel Monteleone in New Orleans.

Voyager

(by Robert Hess, 2006)

- 2 ounces (60ml) rum
- ½ ounce (15ml) lime juice
- ½ ounce (15ml) Bénédictine
- ½ ounce (15ml) falernum
- 2 dashes Angostura bitters

Shake with ice and strain into an ice-filled rocks glass.

Garnish with a lime wedge.

This represents my entry into the classic Tiki cocktail arena. Back in those days, the Polynesian inspired restaurants were intended as a mini-vacation, hence the Voyager name. That, and the fact that I'm also a *Star Trek* fan.

Ward 8

- 2 ounces (60ml) rye whiskey
- ½ ounce (15ml) lemon juice
- ½ ounce (15ml) orange juice
- 1 teaspoon (5ml) grenadine

Shake with ice and strain into a cocktail glass.

Reputedly created in 1898 at the Locke-Ober restaurant in Boston to honor the election of Martin Lomasney to the Massachusetts Senate. Ward 8 refers to Mr. Lomasney's election district. There are problems with this story, but it's close enough for government use.

1900

Whiskey Sour

- 2 ounces (60ml) bourbon whiskey
- 1 ounce (30ml) simple syrup
- ¾ ounce (22ml) lemon juice
- 1 teaspoon (5ml) egg white (optional)

Shake with ice and strain into a small rocks glass or a small wine glass.

This is perhaps the quintessential drink in the sour category. The optional bit of egg white adds a bit of texture as well as a slightly foamy head. Once there was a common sour glass used for this drink. It looked like a cross between a small wine glass and a champagne flute.

Whiskey Sour

White Lady

- •2 ounces (60ml) gin
- •1 ounce (30ml) Cointreau
- •½ ounce (15ml) lemon juice

Shake with ice and strain into a cocktail glass.

White Russian

- •2 ounces (60ml) vodka
- •1 ounce (30ml) coffee liqueur
- •½ ounce (15ml) cream

Pour vodka and coffee liqueur over ice into a rocks glass, then float cream on top.

This is the same as a Black Russian, except with the addition of the float of cream.

White Spider

- •1 ounce (30ml) gin
- •1 ounce (30ml) lemon juice
- •½ ounce (15ml) Cointreau
- •1 teaspoon (5ml) simple syrup

Shake with ice and strain into a cocktail glass.

White Russian

Widow's Kiss

- •2 ounces (60ml) calvados or apple brandy
- •1 ounce (30ml) yellow Chartreuse
- •1 ounce (30ml) Bénédictine
- •1 dash Angostura bitters

Stir with ice and strain into a cocktail glass.

Xeres

- •2 ounces (60ml) sherry
- •1 dash orange bitters
- •1 dash peach bitters

Stir with ice and strain into a cocktail glass.

X.Y.Z.

- •2 ounces (60ml) rum
- •1 ounce (30ml) Cointreau
- •½ ounce (15ml) lemon juice

Shake with ice and strain into a cocktail glass.

This is essentially a rum-based Sidecar. During the Tiki craze, it was referred to as an Outrigger.

Yacht Club

- •¾ ounce (22ml) gin
- •¾ ounce (22ml) sweet vermouth
- •¾ ounce (22ml) orange juice
- •2 dashes Campari
- •2 dashes simple syrup

Shake with ice and strain into a cocktail glass.

Zaza

- •¾ ounce (22ml) gin
- •1½ ounce (45ml) Dubonnet rouge
- •1 dash orange bitters

Stir with ice and strain into a cocktail glass.

This drink most likely dates from around 1900. There was a popular French play at the time called *Zaza* (short for Isabelle), which became both an opera and a film.

1961

Zombie

(Created by Don the Beachcomber)

- 1 ounce (30ml) lemon juice
- 1 ounce (30ml) lime juice
- 1 ounce (30ml) pineapple juice
- 1 teaspoon (5ml) brown sugar
- 1 ounce (30ml) passion fruit syrup
- 1 dash Angostura bitters
- 1 ounce (30ml) gold rum
- 1 ounce (30ml) 151 Demerara rum
- 1 ounce (30ml) white rum

Dissolve sugar in juice.

Shake with ice and pour into a Collins glass.

Garnish with a mint sprig.

This apparently is a real recipe from Don the Beachcomber. It was discovered by Tiki historian Jeff Berry hidden in the pages of Louis Spievak's self-published manual *Barbecue Chef* (1950). In addition to a special acknowledgement to Don, the recipe had a note from Don which read: "I originated and have served this thing since 1934."

Zumbo

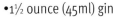

- 1½ ounce (45ml) gin
- ¼ ounce (7ml) Cointreau
- ¼ ounce (7ml) sweet vermouth
- ¼ ounce (7ml) dry vermouth
- 2 dashes Fernet Branca

Stir with ice and strain into a cocktail glass.

Zummy

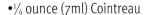

- ¾ ounce (22ml) Bénédictine
- ¾ ounce (22ml) gin
- ½ ounce (15ml) dry vermouth
- ½ ounce (15ml) sweet vermouth
- 1 dash Campari

Stir with ice and strain into a cocktail glass.

1942

Measurement Equivalents

Throughout the recipes in this book I have attempted to use U.S. ounces for all measurements (with English milliliter equivalents), and the odd teaspoon or tablespoon thrown in when that was appropriate for the product being measured. However, there might be times that you will need to convert these measures to something else, or you might come across other recipes which you want to convert to ounces and such. Here are some handy conversion details.

ODD MEASURES:

1 jigger = $1^1/_2$ ounces

1 pony = 1 ounce

1 shot = 1 ounce

1 wineglass = 2 ounces (often used in recipes in the 1800s)

1 drink = $1^1/_2$ to 2 ounces

1 dash = $^1/_{70}{}^{th}$ ounce (approximate)

1 drop = $^1/_{456}{}^{th}$ ounce (approximate)

1 lemon = $1^1/_2$ ounces (average)

1 lime = 1 ounce (average)

1 orange = $2^3/_4$ ounce (average)

1 splash = unknown quantity, use should be avoided

You will also sometimes see *part* used in cocktail recipes. This is intended as a flexible unit of measure in which the ratios of the ingredients are being specified (i.e.: 1 part vermouth, 3 parts gin, 1 dash orange bitters). A recipe using parts should never include specific measurements (ounce, tablespoon, etc), since that wouldn't make sense.

COMMON MEASURES:

1 oz = 6 teaspoons

1 oz = 2 Tablespoons

1 cup = 8 ounces

1 pint = 16 ounces

METRIC MEASURES *(APPROXIMATE)*:

$^1/_4$ ounce = 7ml

$^1/_2$ ounce = 15 ml

$^3/_4$ ounce = 22ml

1 ounce = 30ml

Bibliography

Bergeron, Victor, *Bartender's Guide*, Garden City, 1947

Berry, Jeff, *Sippin' Safari*, Club Tiki Press, 2007

Blue, Anthony, *The Complete Book of Spirits*, Harper Collins, 2004

Boothby, William, *American Bar-Tender*, San Francisco News Company, 1900

Brown, Lorraine, *The Story of Canadian Whiskey*, Fitzhenry & Whiteside, 1994

Calabrese, Salvatore, *Classic Cocktails*, Sterling Publishing, 1997

Difford, Simon, *Cocktails*, diffordsguide, 2005

Embury, David, *The Fine Art of Mixing Drinks*, Doubleday, 1948

Felten, Eric, *How's Your Drink?*, Surrey, 2007

Giglio, Anthony, *Mr. Boston's Platinum Bartender's Guide*, Wiley, 2006

Grossman, Harold, *Grossman's Guide to Wine*, Spirits, and Beers, Charles Scribner's Sons, 1940

Haigh, Ted, *Vintage Spirits & Forgotten Cocktails*, Rockport, 2004

Hess, Robert and Miller, Anistatia, *The Museum of the American Cocktail Pocket Recipe Guide*, Mixellany Press, 2006

Johnson, Harry, *New and Improved Bartender's Manual*, 1900

Jones, Stan, *Jones' Complete Barguide*, Barguide Enterprises, 1977

Lipinski, Robert & Kathleen, *Professional Guide to Alcoholic Beverages*, Van Nostrand Reinhold, 1989

McCaffety, Kerri, *Obituary Cocktail*, Winter Books, 1998

O'Hara, Christopher, *The Bloody Mary*, Lyons Press, 1999

Regan, Gary, *The Joy of Mixology*, Clarkson Potter, 2003

Regan, Gary & Mardee Haidin, *New Classic Cocktails*, Macmillian, 1997

Regan, Gary & Mardee Haidin, *The Book of Bourbon*, Chapters, 1995

Regan, Mardee Haidin, *The Bartender's Best Friend*, Wiley, 2003

Rothbaum, Noah, *The Business of Spirits*, Kaplan, 2007

Thomas, Jerry, *Bartender's Guide*, Dick & Fitzgerald, 1887

Thomas, Jerry, *How To Mix Drinks*, Dick & Fitzgerald, 1862

Wondrich, David, *Imbibe*, Perigree, 2007

Acknowledgements

The author would like to thank everybody who made this book possible. It was a great experience and a wonderful opportunity to be able to pull together all the information necessary to produce this book. Thanks have to start with Gregory Boehm who first envisioned this project and was at the heart of it from the very start. A large component of this book, of course, are the wonderful pictures and illustrations which bring life to its pages. For these I thank Chad Solomon and Christy Pope who painstakingly prepared the cocktails to be wonderfully photographed by Amy K. Sims. Scattered throughout the recipes are also unique creations by many of my cocktailian friends and co-workers around the world: Tony Abou-Ganim, Jamie Boudreau, Kathy Casey, Tito Class, Dale DeGroff, Chris Hannah, Paul Harrington, Bastian Heuser, Francesco Lafranconi, Ryan Magarian, Jim Meehan, Junior Merino, Sean Muldoon, David Nepove, Jonathan Pogash, Gary Regan, Mardee Regan, Charles Schumann, Laurel Semmes, Chad Solomon, Murray Stenson, Gwydion Stone, Chuck Taggart and Charles Tobias.

And I want to specifically thank those people who have specifically been instrumental along my own personal cocktailian journey: Paul Harrington, Ted "Dr. Cocktail" Haigh, Gary Regan, Mardee Haidin Regan, Jason Crume, Kacy Fitch, Ben Dougherty, Murray Stenson, Ryan Magarian, Dale DeGroff, Audrey Saunders, David Wondrich, Chris McMillan, Anistatia Miller, Jared Brown, Cheryl Charming, Simon Ford and Ann Tuennerman.

Photo Credits

Amy K. Sims (pages 2, 5, 55, 57, 96, 98, 101-102, 105, 107-108, 111, 119, 122, 125, 131, 139, 140, 143, 151, page 171, page 177, page 179, page 182, 185, 192, 198, 201, 204, 207)

F. William Lagaret (pages 17, 21, 42, 46-49, 54, 60, 69, 70 (bottom image), 73 (bottom), 75, 77, 79, 81, 86, 89, 91, 117, 141, 147, 152, 157, 175)

Ryan Magarian (pages 121, 144, 180, 194)

Jamie Boudreau (pages 41, 44, 190, 202)

Greg Boehm (pages 152, 189)

Corbis Images: © Helen King/Corbis (page 8); Bettmann/CORBIS, December 29, 1931, Havana Cuba (page 10); © Hulton-Deutsch Collection/CORBIS, June 3, 1926, Westminster, London, England, UK (page 22); Bettmann/CORBIS, ca. 1920s (page 25); Bettmann/CORBIS, January 9, 1951, Chicago, IL, USA (page 43)

Getty Images: Julien Capmeil (page 6)

istockphoto:
Christine Balderas (page 36); Felipe Bello (page 70 (top)); Mike Bentley (page 13); Joe Biafore (page 59); Eugene Bochkarev (page 183); Chelsea Elizabeth Photography (page 124); John Clines (page 173); Richard Gunion (page 76); Danny Hooks (page 129); indykb (page 71 (bottom)); JackJelly (page 176); Zoran Kolundzija (page 94 (bottom right)); Ivan Mateev (pages 127, 136, 146, 158); Steven Miric (page 62 (top)); objectsforall (page 208); Philip Pellat (page 154); George Peters (page 62 (bottom)); Angel Rodríguez (page 174); Gary Sludden (page 162); David Smith (page 169); Klaudia Steiner (pages 94 (top right), 95; 145); Yuri Strakhov (page 73 (top)); Daniel Timiraos (page 63); titelio (page 56); Valentyn Volkov (page 37); *Montage, page 64:* (Row 1, from left) Scott Waite, Larry White, Kevin Russ; (Row 2, from left) Michael Braun, Les Kollegian, Darla Hallmark; (Row 3) David Cannings-Bushell; (Row 4, from left) Mark Wilkinson, Anthony Hall

Jupiter Images: Aladdin Color Inc. (page 211)

StockFood: Cynthia Brown (page 113); Giblin - StockFood Munich (back cover (top), page 30); Amy K. Sims (page 114)

General Index

A

Abou-Ganim, Tony, 135
Absinthe, 90–91
Agave, 77–78
Agavoni, 118
Alaska, 118
Alexander, 118, 119
Algonquin, 120
Amaretto, about, 83
Amer Picon, 91
Americano, 120
Añejo MANhattan, 120–121
Angostura bitters, 89
Ante, 123
Apéritif wines, 90
Armagnac and cognac, about, 68–69
Aromatized wines, 86–88
Aviation, 122, 123

B

Bacardi Cocktail, 123
Balancing flavors, 41, 60
Bamboo, 124
Bar spoons, 48
Bartenders
    appreciation for cocktails, 41
    balancing flavors, 41, 60
    as cocktail "chefs," 31, 39–40
    educating palate, 41
    equipment for. See Tools of the trade
    home, 42–43
    mixology 101, 60–63. See also Ice
    recipes for. See Classic cocktails; Recipes; Index of Recipes by Main Alcoholic Ingredients
    stocking home bars, 58
Bathtub gin, 76
Beach, Don "the Beachcomber," 28, 71, 210
Beach Blanket, 124

Bellini, 124
Bénédictine, 91–92
Bergeron, Victor "Trader Vic," 28, 115, 149, 153, 168
Bermuda Rum Swizzle, 126
Bijou, 125, 126
Bistro Sidecar, 126–127
The Bitter Truth, 90
Bitters
    historical perspective, 16–17, 22–23, 29
    types of, 88–93. See also specific bitters
Black Feather, 127
Black Russian, 127
Blackberry Fizz, 127
Blackstar, 128
Blood and Sand, 128
Bloody Mary, 112–113, 128
Bloomsbury, 129
Bobbo's Bride, 129
Bobby Burns, 129
Bon Vivant's Companion, 20
Bordeaux Cocktail, 129
Boudreau, Jamie, 175, 190, 202
Bourbon, about, 73–74
Bourbon Crusta, 130, 131
Brandy
    about, 68
    cognac and armagnac, 68–69
    drinking, 68
    history of, 68
    pomace brandy, 69
Brandy Cobbler, 130
Brandy Crusta, 130–131
Brandy glasses, 68
Brandy Shrub, 132
Brandy Smash, 132
Bridal, 132
Bronx, 133
Brooklyn, 133
Bucket (rocks) glasses, 52
Bucks, defined, 32
Buck's Fizz, 134
Bull Shot, 134

C

Cabaret, 134
Cable Car, 135
Cachaça, 71
Caesar, 135
Caipirinha, 136
Calvados Cocktail, 136
Campari, 92
Canadian whisky, about, 71, 74
Canton, 137
Caprice, 137
Captain's Blood, 137
Casey, Kathy, 126
Casino, 137
Cecchini, Toby, 104
Champagne Antoine, 137
Champagne Cocktail, 138, 139
Champagne Flamingo, 138
Champagne glasses (flutes and coupes), 51
Champs Elysées, 138
Channel knives, 54
Chaplin, 138
Chartreuse, 92
Chas, 138
Chilling drinks and glassware, 45, 61
Chimney (Collins) glasses, 52
Chrysanthemum Cocktail, 141
Class, Tito, 129
Classic cocktails, 97–115
    Bloody Mary, 112–113, 128
    Classic Martini, 108, 109, 170
    Cosmopolitan, 104–105, 145
    Daiquiri, 100–101, 146
    Mai Tai, 114, 115, 168
    Manhattan, 110–111, 169
    Margarita, 102, 103, 169
    Old Fashioned, 106–107, 177
    Sidecar, 98, 99, 194
Classic Martini, 108, 109
Cloister, 141
Clover Club, 140, 141
Cobblers
    defined, 32

Index of Recipes by Main Alcoholic Ingredients

About the Author

Robert Hess lives and works in Seattle, Washington. He traces his interest in the cocktail to a childhood fascination of bartenders, who effortlessly transformed the contents of the bottles around them into gleaming jewels of refreshment. Eventually, he took action on these early memories, absorbing all he could about the classic art of mixology. Using his culinary training as a canvas, he views cocktails as a cuisine with the same artistic flavor potentials as the food prepared by a gourmet French chef. He has since become a ceaseless evangelist of quality cocktails, working with restaurants, bartenders and consumers to help them better understand how to advance their craft.

He created DrinkBoy.com and its associated discussion forum to allow bartenders around the world to interact with each other and share any thoughts, ideas and experiences that would benefit everybody through an open discussion. He has since teamed up with several others across the country to found The Museum of the American Cocktail (www.MuseumOfTheAmericanCocktail.org). Coinciding with the Museum's opening exhibits in New Orleans and New York will be a variety of events and seminars around the world.

He also is the host and executive producer of *The Cocktail Spirit* a web-based video series being presented through the Small Screen Network (www.SmallScreenNetwork.com). His videos provide easily accessed information and instructions on how anybody can make great cocktails.